歓　迎

Titles in this series:

Just Enough **Japanese**

R.Ahlberg, T.Ando, T.Boardman, D.L.Ellis

Pronunciation **Dr J.Baldwin**

Introduction **Peter Milward, SJ**

PASSPORT BOOKS
NTC/Contemporary Publishing Group

This edition first published in 1985 by Passport Books
A division of NTC/Contemporary Publishing Group, Inc.
4255 West Touhy Avenue
Lincolnwood (Chicago), Illinois 60646-1975 U.S.A.
Copyright © 1984 by R. Ahlberg, T. Ando, T. Boardman, D.L. Ellis
Originally published by Pan Books
Printed in the United States of America
International Standard Book Number: 0-8442-9510-8
99 00 01 02 03 QP 21 20 19 18 17 16 15 14 13 12 11 10 9

Contents

Using the phrase book

- This phrase book is designed to help you get by in Japan, to get what you want or need. It concentrates on the simplest but most effective way you can express these needs in an unfamiliar language.
- The CONTENTS on p. 5 gives you a good idea of which section to consult for the phrase you need.
- The INDEX on p. 189 gives more detailed information about where to look for your phrase.
- When you have found the right page you will be given:
  either—the exact phrase
  or   —help in making up a suitable sentence
  and   —help to get the pronunciation right
- The English sentences in **bold type** will be useful for you in a variety of different situations, so they are worth learning by heart. (See also DO IT YOURSELF, p. 177)
- Wherever possible you will find help in understanding what Japanese people are saying to *you*, in reply to your questions.
- If you want to practice the basic nuts and bolts of the language further, look at the DO IT YOURSELF section starting on p. 177.
- Note especially these two sections:
  Everyday expressions, p. 13
  Shop talk, p. 69
  You are sure to want to refer to them most frequently.
- Once abroad, remember to make good use of the local tourist offices (see p. 30).

U.S. Addresses

Japan National Tourist Organization (JNTO)

1 Rockefeller Plaza, Suite 1250	401 N. Michigan Ave.
New York, NY 10020	Suite 770
(212) 757-5640	Chicago, IL 60611
	(312) 222-0874

515 S. Figueroa St., Suite 1470
Los Angeles, CA 90071
(213) 623-1952

Japan Travel Bureau USA Inc.

810 7th Ave.	2050 W 190th St., Suite 108
New York, NY 10019	Torrence, CA 90504
(212) 698-4900	(310) 618-0961

A note on the pronunciation systems and the Japanese language

This book contains two English transcriptions of the Japanese. The first is a specially designed system to help with pronunciation. The second is a standard system (Hepburn) which you may meet in dictionaries, grammars and other English books about Japan, but which is not strictly a guide to the pronunciation of the language.

The pronunciation system in this book is founded on three assumptions: firstly, that it is not possible to describe in print the sounds of a foreign language in such a way that the English speaker with no phonetic training will produce them accurately, or even intelligibly; secondly, that perfect pronunciation is not essential for communication, and lastly that the average visitor abroad is more interested in achieving successful communication than in learning how to pronounce new speech sounds. Observation and experience have shown these assumptions to be justified.

The most important characteristic of the present system, therefore, is that it makes no attempt whatsoever to teach the sounds of the other language, but uses instead the nearest English sounds to them. The sentences transcribed for pronunciation are designed to be read as naturally as possible, as if they were ordinary English (of a generally south-eastern English variety), and with no attempt to make the words sound 'foreign'. In this way you will still sound quite American, but you will at the same time be understood. Practice always helps performance, and it is a good idea to rehearse aloud any of the sentences you know you are going to need. When you do come to the point of using them, say them with conviction. Try to read the phoneticized Japanese as *quickly* and smoothly as you can, *without* pausing over the hyphens.

In Japanese it is important to read each syllable with equal emphasis. For instance, in the following English example we have ten syllables and ten stresses: Little Jack Horner sat in the corner. Though this will probably sound rather mechanical to an English ear, it will help the Japanese speaker to understand you.

Of course you may enjoy trying to pronounce a foreign language as well as possible and the present system is a good way to start. However, since it only uses the sounds of English, you will very soon need to depart from it as you begin to imitate the sounds you hear the native speaker produce.

There are various levels of politeness built into the actual grammar of Japanese. This book uses the neutral polite (or masu-desu) form throughout. The use of more elevated forms of honorifics is slowly declining and the neutral polite form has become the standard form of address between people who are strangers to each other.

Three scripts are needed to write Japanese: Chinese characters and two syllabary scripts developed by the Japanese from Chinese characters (hiragana and katakana, the latter being used mainly for words of foreign origin). All three scripts are used throughout this book in the normal Japanese manner.

The order of the Japanese sentence is usually quite different from the English. For example: 'Please can you repeat that?' would be 'Repeat please can you?' and a more complex sentence: 'Where does the bus for the airport leave from?' would be 'For the airport bus where does leave from?' In this book the position of the three dots (...) will help you with the correct order.

Introduction

English-speaking people are apt to feel out of place when travelling in a foreign country — especially where the inhabitants speak a foreign language. Still, if it is somewhere in Europe, they may well recognize some of the words, as somehow related to their own English words. But in Japan they find themselves linguistically altogether at sea. Nowadays, it is true, many English words have been incorporated into Japanese — at least ten thousand, at a conservative estimate; but they are spelled and pronounced by the Japanese in a manner that is quite unrecognizable to the inexperienced traveller. As for the traditional Japanese words, they have no linguistic connection with European words at all. The only way for the traveller in Japan is to equip himself with a conveniently portable word-book and to familiarize himself with the most common and most practical expressions. Even so, only practice — and patience — will make him at all perfect.

All the same, it may be comforting to know that, once the basic words are memorized, spoken Japanese isn't so very difficult: the main problems are with reading and writing — which are of little concern to the traveller. Japanese grammar is even easier than English grammar; and as for the pronunciation, it isn't so difficult for those who have some familiarity with pure vowels. The important thing to remember is that there are only five vowels in Japanese: a, i, u, e, o — in that order. As for the consonants, they have to be pronounced much more delicately than we do in English, passing ever so lightly over d's and t's, and blowing between the lips to produce f's (as in Fuji). It is also helpful, in speaking, to move the lips as little as possible.

Just Enough Japanese, takes the bull of pronunciation by the horns, from an English point of view, presenting the words not only in their customary (Hepburn) romanization but also in an Anglicized form. This is one obvious and useful feature; but it isn't the only one. No less useful are the phrases, chosen for their practical value to the English-speaking traveller. What is more, the 'cultural' context within which the phrases are to be used is aptly anticipated at the beginning of each section under the heading *Essential information*. These three points taken together will surely make this book an ideal travellers' companion in Japan.

Peter Milward, SJ
Sophia University,
Tokyo

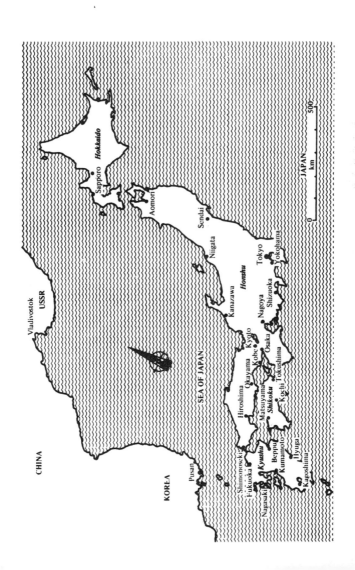

Everyday expressions

[See also 'Shop talk', p. 69]

Hello	こんにちは kon-nee-chee-wa konnichi wa
Good morning	おはようございます o-ha-yaw goz-eye-mass ohayō gozaimasu
Good afternoon] Good day]	こんにちは kon-nee-chee-wa konnichi wa
Good evening	こんばんは kom-ban-wa komban wa
Good night	おやすみなさい o-yass-oo-mee nass-eye oyasumi nasai
Good-bye	さようなら sye-aw-narra sayōnara
See you later	じゃ また ja matta ja mata
Yes	はい high hai
Please	お願いします on-eg-eye shee-mass onegai shimasu
Yes, please	はい お願いします high on-eg-eye shee-mass hai onegai shimasu
Great!	いいですね ee-dess nair ii desu ne
Thank you	ありがとうございます arry-gattaw goz-eye-mass arigatō gozaimasu

Thank you very much   どうも　ありがとうございます
daw-maw arry-gattaw goz-eye-mass
dōmo arigatō gozaimasu

That's right   そうですね
saw dess nair
sō desu ne

No   いいえ
ee-ay
iie

No, thank you   いいえ　結構です
ee-ay kek-kaw dess
iie kekkō desu

I disagree   私は　そう思いません
wattash-ee wa saw om-oy-mass-en
watashi wa sō omoimasen

Excuse me ⎤
Sorry ⎦   すみません
soo-mee-mass-en
sumimasen

Don't mention it ⎤
That's OK ⎦   どういたしまして
daw ee-tash-ee mash-tay
dō itashimashite

That's good ⎤
I like it ⎦   いいですね
ee dess nair
ii desu ne

That's no good ⎤
I don't like it ⎦   よくないですね
yok-oo nye dess nair
yoku nai desu ne

I know   わかっています
wakkattem-ass
wakatte imasu

I don't know   知りません
shee-ree-mass-en
shirimasen

It doesn't matter   かまいません
kam-eye-mass-en
kamaimasen

Where's the toilet, please?   トイレはどこですか
toy-ray wa dokko dess ka
toire wa doko desu ka

How much is that? [*point*]
それはいくらですか
sorray wa ee-koorra dess ka
sore wa ikura desu ka

Is the service included?
サービス料がはいっていますか
sah-beess-ree-aw ga height-tem-ass ka
sābisu ryō ga haitte imasu ka

Do you speak English?
英語ができますか
ay-gaw ga dek-ee-mass ka
eigo ga dekimasu ka

I'm sorry...
すみませんが……
soo-mee-mass-en ga...
sumimasen ga...

I don't speak Japanese
日本語が話せません
nee-hon-go ga hanass-em-ass-en
nihongo ga hanasemasen

I speak only a little Japanese
日本語がすこししか話せません
nee-hon-go ga skosh-ee shka hanass-em-ass-en
nihongo ga sukoshi shika hanasemasen

I don't understand
わかりません
wakka-ree-mass-en
wakarimasen

Please can you...
……ください
...koo-dass-eye
...kudasai

repeat that?
くりかえして
koo-ree-kye shtay
kurikaeshite

speak more slowly?
もっとゆっくり話して
mot-taw yook-oo-ree hanash-tay
motto yukkuri hanashite

write it down?
書いて
kye-tay
kaite

What is this called in Japanese? [*point*]
これは日本語でなんといいますか
korray wa nee-hon-goddair nan-toh ee-mass ka
kore wa nihongo de nan to iimasu ka

Entering the country

ESSENTIAL INFORMATION

- Don't waste time just before you leave rehearsing what you're going to say to the officials at the port or airport—the chances are that you won't have to say anything at all, especially if you travel by air.
- It's more useful to check that you have your documents handy for the journey: passport, tickets, money, traveler's checks, insurance documents, and driver's license.
- You may be asked routine questions by the customs officials [*see below*]. If you have to give personal details see 'Meeting people', p. 18. The other important answer to know is 'Nothing': なにもありません (nan-ee maw arry-mass-en/nani mo arimasen).

ROUTINE QUESTIONS

Passport?	パスポートは passpawto wa pasupōto
Insurance?	保険は hokken wa hoken wa
Ticket, please	切符をみせてください keep-poo o mee-set-ay koo-dass-eye kippu o misete kudasai
Have you anything to declare?	なにか申告するものがありますか nan-ee-ka sheen-kok sroo-monno ga arry-mass ka nanika shinkoku suru mono ga arimasu ka
Where are you going?	どこへ行くんですか dokko ay ee-koon dess ka doko e iku n desu ka
How long are you staying?	どのぐらいいる予定ですか donno goo-rye irroo yaw-tay dess ka dono gurai iru yotei desu ka

Where are you staying?	どこに泊まりますか dokko nee tom-arry-mass ka doko ni tomarimasu ka
Where have you come from?	どこから来ましたか dokko karra kee-mash-ta ka doko kara kimashita ka

You may also have to fill in forms which ask for:

surname	姓
first name	名まえ
maiden name	旧姓
date of birth	生年月日
place of birth	出生地
address	住所
nationality	国籍
profession	職業
passport number	旅券番号
issued at	発行地
signature	自署

Meeting people

[*See also 'Everyday expressions', p. 13*]

Breaking the ice

Hello	こんにちは kon-nee-chee-wa konnichi wa
Good morning	おはようございます o-ha-yaw goz-eye-mass ohayō gozaimasu
How are you?	お元気ですか o-ghen-kee dess ka ogenki desu ka
Pleased to meet you	どうぞよろしく daw-zaw yorrosh-koo dōzo yoroshiku
I am here...	……きています ...kee-tay-ee-mass ...kite imasu
on vacation	休暇で kew-kaddair kyūka de
on business	仕事で shee-gottaw-dair shigoto de
Can I offer you...	……はいかがですか ...wa ee-kaggad-ess ka ...wa ikaga desu ka
a drink?	飲みもの nom-ee monno nomimono
a cigarette?	タバコ tabbak-aw tabako
a cigar?	葉巻 ham-ak-ee hamaki

Are you staying long?	どのぐらい いらっしゃいますか donno goo-rye ee-rash-eye-mass ka dono gurai irrasshaimasu ka

Name

What's your name?	お名前はなんですか onna-my wa nan dess ka onamae wa nan desu ka
My name is...	私は……です wattash-ee wa...dess watashi wa...desu

Family

Are you married?	結婚していますか kek-kon shtay-ee-mass ka kekkon shite imasu ka
I am...	私は…… wattash-ee wa... watashi wa...
married	結婚しています kek-kon shtay-ee-mass kekkon shite imasu
single	独身です dok-shin dess dokushin desu
This is...	こちらは……です ko-cheerra wa...dess kochira wa...desu
my wife	家内 kan-eye kanai
my husband	主人 shoo-jeen shujin
my daughter	娘 moo-soo-may musume
my son	息子 mooss-koh musuko

This is...

こちらは……です
ko-cheerra wa...dess
kochira wa...desu

    my (boy/girl) friend

友だち
tom-oddatch-ee
tomodachi

    my (male/female)
     colleague

同僚
daw-ree-aw
dōryō

Do you have any children?

子どもさんがいますか
kod-ommo san ga ee-mass ka
kodomo san ga imasu ka

I have...

……います
...ee-mass
...imasu

    one daughter

娘がひとり
moo-soo-may ga shtorry
musume ga hitori

    one son

息子がひとり
mooss-koh ga shtorry
musuko ga hitori

    two daughters

娘がふたり
moo-soo-may ga f-tarry
musume ga futari

    three sons

息子が三人
mooss-koh ga san-neen
musuko ga sannin

No, I haven't any children

いいえ 子どもはいません
ee-ay, kod-ommo wa ee-mass-en
iie kodomo wa imasen

Where you live

Are you...

あなたは……ですか
an-atta wa...dess ka
anata wa...desu ka

    Japanese?

日本人
nee-hon-jeen
nihonjin

    Chinese?

中国人
choo-gok-oo-jeen
chūgokujin

Korean?	韓国人 kan-kok-oo-jeen kankokujin
I am...	私は……です wattash-ee wa...dess watashi wa...desu
English	イギリス人 ee-ghee-reesser-jeen igirisujin
Australian	オーストラリア人 awss-taw-rall-yaj-een ōsutorariajin
American	アメリカ人 am-ellee-ka-jeen amerikajin
Canadian [*For other nationalities,* *see p. 170*]	カナダ人 kan-adda-jeen kanadajin

Where you are from

I've come...	……きました ...kee-mash-ta ...kimashita
from London	ロンドンから lon-don karra rondon kara
from England [*For other countries,* *see p. 168*]	イギリスから ee-ghee-reess karra igirisu kara

For the businessman and woman

I'm from...(firm's name)	……のものです ...no monno dess ...no mono desu
I have an appointment with...	……とお約束があります ...toh o-yak-sok-oo ga arry-mass ...to oyakusoku ga arimasu
May I speak to...	……お願いします ...on-eg-eye shee-mass ...onegai shimasu

This is my card

これは名刺です
korray wa may-shee dess
kore wa meishi desu

I'm sorry I'm late

おそくなってすみません
ossok-oo nat-tay soo-mee-mass-en
osoku natte sumimasen

Can I make another appointment?

また会っていただけますか
matta at-tay ee-taddak-em-ass ka
mata atte itadakemasu ka

I'm staying at the (Tokyo) hotel

東京ホテルに泊っています
tawk-yaw ho-terroo-nee tom-at-tay-ee-mass
tōkyō hoteru ni tomatte imasu

I'm staying in (Harumi) Street

(晴海) 通りにいます
(harroo-mee) daw-ree-nee ee-mass
(harumi) dōri ni imasu

Asking the way

WHAT TO SAY

Excuse me, please

すみません
soo-mee-mass-en
sumimasen

How do I get...

…どうやっていけばいいですか
...daw yat-tay ee-kebba ee dess ka
...dō yatte ikeba ii desu ka

to Osaka?

大阪へは
aw-sakka-ay wa
ōsaka e wa

to Meiji Street?

明治通りへは
may-jee daw-ree-ay-wa
meiji dōri e wa

to the (Sakura) hotel?

さくらホテルへは
(sak-oo-ra) ho-terroo-ay-wa
(sakura) hoteru e wa

to the airport?	空港へは
	koo-kaw-ay-wa
	kūkō e wa
to the beach?	海水浴場へは
	kye-see-yok-oo-jaw-ay-wa
	kaisuiyokujō e wa
to the bus station?	バスターミナルへは
	bass-tah-mee-na-roo-ay-wa
	basu tāminaru e wa
to the historic site?	史跡へは
	shee-sek-ee-ay-wa
	shiseki e wa
to the market?	市へは
	ee-chee-ay-wa
	ichi e wa
to the police station?	警察署へは
	kay-sats-shaw-ay-wa
	keisatsusho e wa
to the port?	港へは
	mee-nat-o-ay-wa
	minato e wa
to the post office?	郵便局へは
	yoo-beenk-yok-oo-ay-wa
	yūbinkyoku e wa
to the railway station?	駅へは
	ek-ee-ay-wa
	eki e wa
to the sports stadium?	スタジアムへは
	staj-ee-am-oo-ay-wa
	sutajiamu e wa
to the tourist information office?	旅行者案内所へは
	ree-aw-kaw-sha an-nye-jaw-ay-wa
	ryokōsha annaijo e wa
to the town centre?	繁華街へは
	han-kag-eye-ay-wa
	hankagai e wa
to the town hall?	市役所へは
	shee-ak-shaw-ay-wa
	shiyakusho e wa
Excuse me, please	すみません
	soo-mee-mass-en
	sumimasen

Is there ... near by?　……は近くにありますか

...wa ch-kak-oo-nee arry-mass ka

...wa chikaku ni arimasu ka

an art gallery	美術館
	bee-joots-kan
	bijutsukan
a bakery	パン屋
	pan-ya
	panya
a bank	銀行
	gheen-kaw
	ginkō
a bar	バー
	bar
	bā
a botanical garden	植物園
	shok-oo-boots-oo-en
	shokubutsuen
a bus stop	バス停
	bass-tay
	basutei
a butcher shop	肉屋
	nee-koo-ya
	nikuya
a café	喫茶店
	keess-atten
	kissaten
a cake shop	ケーキ屋
	kair-kee-ya
	kēkiya
a campsite	キャンプ場
	kee-amp-jaw
	kyampujō
a car park	駐車場
	choo-sha-jaw
	chūshajō
a change bureau/ currency exchange	両替所
	ree-aw-gye-jaw
	ryōgaejo
a chemist's/drugstore	薬屋
	k-soo-ree-ya
	kusuriya

a church	教会 kee-aw-kye kyōkai
a cinema/movie theater	映画館 ay-ga-kan eigakan
a dentist's	歯医者 high-sha haisha
a department store	デパート dep-art-o depāto
a disco	ディスコ dee-sko disko
a doctor's office	医者 ee-sha isha
a dry cleaner's ⎤ a laundry ⎦	クリーニング屋 koo-reen-eeng-oo-ya kurīninguya
a fish store	魚屋 sak-anna-ya sakanaya
a garage (for repairs)	ガレージ ga-rair-jee garēji
a greengrocer's	八百屋 ya-o-ya yaoya
a grocer's	食料品店 shok-oo-ree-aw-heen-ten shokuryōhinten
a hairdresser's (women)	美容院 bee-yaw-een biyōin
hairdresser's (men)	散髪屋 sanpatsuya sampatsu-ya
a hardware shop	金物屋 kanna-monno-ya kanamonoya

Is there ... near by?

…は近くにありますか
…wa ch-kak-oo-nee arry-mass ka
…wa chikaku ni arimasu ka

a hospital
病院
b-yaw-een
byōin

a hotel
ホテル
ho-terroo
hoteru

a museum
博物館
hak-oo-boots-kan
hakubutsukan

a night club
ナイトクラブ
night-o koo-rab-oo
naitokurabu

a park
公園
kaw-en
kōen

a petrol/gas station
ガソリンスタンド
gass-o-leen stand-o
gasorin sutando

a post box/mailbox
ポスト
poss-toh
posuto

a public telephone
公衆電話
kaw-shoo-den-wa
kōshū denwa

a restaurant
レストラン
rest-o-ran
resutoran

a shrine
神社
jeen-ja
jinja

a snack bar
食堂
shok-oo-daw
shokudō

a sports ground
運動場
oon-daw-jaw
undōjō

a supermarket
スーパーマーケット
soo-par-mar-ket-taw
sūpāmāketto

a sweet shop/candy store	お菓子屋 o-kash-ee-ya okashiya
a swimming pool	プール poo-loo pūru
a taxi stand	タクシー乗り場 tak-shee norreebba takushī noriba
a temple	お寺 o-terra otera
a theater	劇場 ghek-ee-jaw gekijō
a tobacconist's/smoke shop	タバコ屋 tabbak-aw-ya tabakoya
a toilet	トイレ toy-ray toire
a travel agent's	旅行会社 ree-aw-kaw-gye-sha ryokōgaisha
a youth hostel	ユースホステル yooss-hoss-terroo yūsuhosuteru
a zoo	動物園 daw-boots-oo-en dōbutsuen

DIRECTIONS

Left	左 hee-da-ree hidari
Right	右 mee-ghee migi
Straight on	まっすぐ mass-oo-goo massugu

There	あそこ
	ass-okko
	asoko
First left/right	次の角を左/右に
	tsoo-ghee no kaddo-o hee-da-ree/ mee-ghee nee
	tsugi no kado o hidari/ migi ni
Second left/right	二番目の角を左/右に
	nee ban-may-no-kaddo o hee-da-ree/mee-ghee nee
	nibanme no kado o hidari/ migi ni
At the crossroads	交差点で
	kaw-sat-en dair
	kōsaten de
At the traffic lights	信号で
	sheen-gaw dair
	shingō de
At the level-crossing	踏み切りで
	foo-mee-kee-ree dair
	fumikiri de
It's near/far	近い/遠いです
	ch-kye/taw-ee dess
	chikai/tōi desu
One kilometre	一キロ
	ee-chee-kee-law
	ichi kiro
Two kilometres	二キロ
	nee kee-law
	ni kiro
Five minutes...	五分
	gaw-foon
	gohun
on foot	歩いて
	arree-tay
	aruite
by car	車で
	koo-roo-maddair
	kuruma de

Take...	……に乗ってください
	...nee not-tay koo-dass-eye
	...ni notte kudasai
the bus	バス
	bass-oo
	basu
the train	電車
	den-sha
	densha
the underground/subway	地下鉄
[*For public transport,*	ch-kattets
see p. 140]	chikatetsu

The tourist information office

ESSENTIAL INFORMATION

- There is no standard tourist sign or symbol in Japan.
- **JNTO** (Japan National Tourist Organization). This is a non-profit government office which provides information only on accommodation, transport, fares, theatres and other aspects of possible interest to the visitor to Japan. Information, brochures, etc. are free of charge. They do not make reservations.
- **JTB** (Japan Travel Bureau). An agency which provides information and makes reservations for accommodation, railway tickets, airline tickets, bus tours and package tours (English-speaking guides).
- Both of these organizations have English-speaking sections and information is available from the following telephone numbers:
  JNTO Tokyo (03) 502 – 1461
  JTB　Tokyo (03) 274 – 0042
- Travel offices can also be found at airports and at some railway stations, shopping centres and department stores but the language (spoken and written) is likely to be Japanese.
- English language newspapers and magazines are also a useful source of information for tourist information. The newspapers are sold at most station kiosks in the large towns and cities: the magazines can also be obtained from **JNTO** and **JTB**.
- For finding a tourist office, see p. 22.

WHAT TO SAY

Please, have you got..	……が ありますか
	...ga arry-mass ka
	... ga arimasu ka
a plan of the town?	町の地図
	match-ee no chee-zoo
	machi no chizu
a list of hotels?	ホテルのリスト
	ho-terroo no-leesto
	hoteru no risuto
a list of campsites?	キャンプ場のリスト
	kee-amp-jaw-no-leesto
	kyampujō no risuto

a list of coach excursions?	観光バスのリスト kankaw-bass-no-leesto kankō basu no risuto
a list of restaurants?	レストランのリスト restoh-ran-no-leesto resutoran no risuto
a list of events?	催し物のリスト mo-yaw-shee-monno-no-leesto moyōshimono no risuto
a leaflet on the town?	町についての案内書 matchee-nee-tseetay-no 　an-nye-shaw machi ni tsuite no 　annaisho
a leaflet on the region?	この地方についての案内書 konno cheehaw-nee-tseetay-no 　an-nye-shaw kono chihō ni tsuite no 　annaisho
a railway timetable?	列車の時刻表 resh-ya no jeekok-hee-aw ressha no jikokuhyō
a bus timetable?	バスの時刻表 bass no jeekok-hee-aw basu no jikokuhyō
In English, please	英語でお願いします ay-go day on-eg-eye sheemas eigo de onegai shimasu
How much do I owe you?	いくら払えばいいですか ee-koorra harrye-ebba ee dess ka ikura haraeba ii desu ka
Can you recommend...	……を教えてください ...o oshee-ettay koo-dass-eye ...o oshiete kudasai
a cheap hotel?	安いホテル yassee ho-terroo yasui hoteru
a cheap restaurant?	安いレストラン yassee resto-ran yasui resutoran
Can you make a booking for me?	予約してくれますか yoy-ak-oo shtay koo-ray mass ka yoyaku shite kuremasu ka

LIKELY ANSWERS

No	ありません/ないです
	arry-mass-en/nye dess
	arimasen/nai desu
I'm sorry	すみません
	soo-mee-mass-en
	sumimasen
I don't have a list of campsites	キャンプ場のリストはありません
	kee-amp-jaw-no leesto wa arry-mass-en
	kyampujō no risuto wa arimasen
I haven't got any left	もうありません/ないです
	maw arry-mass-en/nye dess
	mō arimasen/nai desu
It's free	無料です
	moo-ree-aw-dess
	muryō desu

Accommodation
Hotel

ESSENTIAL INFORMATION

- If you want hotel-type accommodation, all the following words are worth looking for on name boards:
  ホテル　　　(hotel)
  旅館　　　　(Japanese inn)
  民宿　　　　(a room in a private house)
  国民宿舎　　(National Lodge)
  国民休暇村　(People's Holiday Village)
- Names of Western-style hotels are usually written in Roman letters but sometimes Japanese letters are used.
- Lists of hotels, both Western-style and Japanese-style, can be obtained from local tourist offices or the Japan Travel Bureaus in New York, Chicago, and L.A. (see p. 7).
- Most Western-style hotels are comparable in cost with those in the U.S. and Europe, ranging from inexpensive business hotels to deluxe international hotels. English is usually spoken.
- Some of the larger hotels are small cities unto themselves, with shopping arcades, a variety of restaurants and bars, secretarial and photocopy services, and a variety of other conveniences.
- Rooms are generally smaller than their European counterparts. Costs are for the rooms themselves (not per person) and meals are not included. If there's a small fridge in the room, the drinks inside must be paid for separately. Some of the larger hotels also have Japanese-style rooms. Tipping is unnecessary as a 10% tax and 10% service charge is usually added to your bill.
- There are various different kinds of Japanese-style hotels, but in all of them you must be prepared to take off your shoes upon entering, sleep on a Japanese style bed on the floor and sit on the floor for meals (usually Japanese cuisine, breakfast and dinner included in the price of the room).
- A Japanese breakfast is likely to consist of tea, rice, raw fish and pickle.
- 旅館　(ryokan—Japanese inns). Rates can be as or more expensive than Western-style hotels but the service is excellent.
- 国民休暇村 (People's Holiday Villages). These are large scale

recreation and lodging facilities located within national parks.
Reservations must be made well in advance through your travel
agent or the Japan Travel Bureau.
- 国民宿舎 (National Lodges). Basically the same as above but on a
  smaller scale. There are many more of these than the People's
  Holiday Villages, but again advance booking is necessary.
- 民宿 (a room in a private house). Many of these are run by fam-
  ilies around the country particularly in areas with tourist attrac-
  tions. The TIC will probably have a list of rooms available and
  may also provide information on etiquette in a Japanese home.
  Similar to these are 'pensions' a kind of boarding-house but more
  Western than Japanese: 貸別荘 (kash-ee-bess-saw/kashi bessō)
  where one rents a whole house/cabin.

WHAT TO SAY

I have a booking	予約してあります
	yoy-ak-oo shtay arry-mass
	yoyaku shite arimasu
Have you any vacancies, please?	部屋がありますか
	heyya ga arry-mass ka
	heya ga arimasu ka
Can I book a room?	部屋を予約したいのですが
	heyya o yoy-ak-oo shtie no dess ga
	heya o yoyaku shitai no desu ga
It's for one person	ひとりです
	shtorry dess
	hitori desu
It's for two persons [*For numbers, see p. 154*]	ふたりです
	f-tarry dess
	futari desu
It's for...	……です
	...dess
	...desu
one night	一泊
	eep-pak-oo
	ippaku
two nights	二泊
	nee hak-oo
	nihaku

one week	·週間 eesh-shoo-kan isshūkan
two weeks	·週間 nee shoo-kan nishūkan
I'd like...	……お願いしたいのですが ...o-neg-eye-shtie-no dess ga ...onegai shitai no desu ga
a room	·部屋 shtoh heyya hitoheya
two rooms	·部屋 f-ta heyya futaheya
a room with a single bed	シングル ·部屋 sheen-goo-roo shtoh heyya shinguru hitoheya
a room with two single beds	ツイン ·部屋 tsoo-ween shtoh heyya tsuin hitoheya
a room with a double bed	ダブル一部屋 dab-oo-roo shtoh heyya daburu hitoheya
I'd like a room...	……部屋がほしいんです ...heyya ga hosh-een dess ...heya ga hoshii n desu
with a toilet	トイレ付きの toy-ret-skee no toire-tsuki no
with a bathroom	風呂付きの foo-raw-tskee no furo-tsuki no
with a shower	シャワー付きの sha-wa-tskee no shawā-tsuki no
with a cot	子ども用ベッド付きの kod-ommo yaw beddo tskee no kodomo yō beddo-tsuki no
with a view	ながめのいい nag-am-ay no ee nagame no ii

I'd like...

……がいいんですが
...ga een dess ga
...ga ii n desu ga

   full board

三食付き
san-shok-oot-skee
sanshoku-tsuki

   bed and breakfast
   [*See essential information*]

朝食付き
chaw-shok-oot-skee
chōshoku-tsuki

Do you serve meals?

食事ができますか
shok-oo-jee ga dek-ee-mass ka
shokuji ga dekimasu ka

At what time is...

……は何時ですか
...wa nan-jee dess ka
...wa nanji desu ka

   breakfast?

朝食
chaw-shok-oo
chōshoku

   lunch?

昼食
choo-shok-oo
chūshoku

   dinner?

夕食
yoo-shok-oo
yūshoku

How much is it?

いくらですか
ee-koorra dess ka
ikura desu ka

Can I look at the room?

部屋を見せてもらえますか
heyya o mee-set-ay morra-em-ass
  ka
heya o misete moraemasu ka

OK, I'll take it

いいですね。これにします
ee dess nair korray nee shee-mass
ii desu ne. kore ni shimasu

No thanks, I won't take it

残念ながらけっこうです
zan-nen-nag-arra kek-kaw dess
zannennagara kekkō desu

I'd prefer a room...

……部屋のほうがいいのですが
...heyya no haw ga ee no dess ga
...heya no hō ga ii no desu ga

at the front/at the back	表側の 裏側の
	ommot-ay ga-wa no/oo-rag-awwa no
	omotegawa no/uragawa no
The key to number (10), please	(10) 番の鍵お願いします
	(joo) ban no kag-ee on-eg-eye-shee mass
	(jū) ban no kagi onegai shimasu
Please, may I have...	……をいただけますか
	...o ee-taddak-em-ass ka
	...o itadakemasu ka
a coat hanger?	ハンガー
	han-ga
	hangā
a towel?	タオル
	ta-or-oo
	taoru
a glass?	コップ
	kop-oo
	koppu
some soap?	せっけん
	sek-ken
	sekken
an ashtray?	灰皿
	high-zarra
	haizara
another pillow?	枕をもうひとつ
	mak-oorra o maw shtots
	makura o mō hitotsu
another blanket?	毛布をもうひとつ
	maw-foo o maw shtots
	mōfu o mō hitotsu
Come in!	どうぞ
	daw-zaw
	dōzo
One moment, please!	ちょっとまってください
	chot-taw mat-tay koo-dass-eye
	chotto matte kudasai

Please can you...

……いただけますか
...ee-taddak-em-ass ka
...itadakemasu ka

  do this laundry?

これをクリーニングして
korray o koo-ree-neeng-oo shtay
kore o kurīningu shite

  call me at...?

……に呼んで
...nee yon-day
...ni yonde

  help me with my luggage?

荷物を運ぶのをてつだって
nee-mots o hak-ob-oo no o
    tet-soo-dat-tay
nimotsu o hakobu no o
    tetsudatte

  call me a taxi for...?
[*For times, see p. 158*]

……へ行くのにタクシーを呼んで
...ay ee-koo non-ee tak-shee o
    yon-day
...e iku noni takushī o
    yonde

The bill, please

お勘定お願いします
o-kan-jaw on-eg-eye-shee-mass
okanjō onegai shimasu

Is service included?

サービス料ははいっていますか
sah-beess ree-aw wa
    high-tay-ee-mass ka
sābisuryō wa haitte imasu ka

I think this is wrong

これはまちがっていると思います
korray wa match-eeng-at-tay-
    ee-roo tom-oy-mass
kore wa machigatte iru
    to omoimasu

May I have a receipt?

領収書をください
ree-aw-shoo-shaw o koo-dass-eye
ryōshūsho o kudasai

At breakfast

Some more..., please

……をもうすこしください
...o maw skosh-ee koo-dass-sye
...o mō sukoshi kudasai

  coffee

コーヒー
kaw-hee
kōhī

tea	紅茶
	kaw-chah
	kōcha
bread	パン
	pan
	pan
butter	バター
	bat-ah
	batā
jam	ジャム
	jam-oo
	jamu

May I have a Western-style breakfast?

西洋式の朝食ができますか

say-yawsh-kee no chaw-shok-oo ga dek-ee-mass ka

seiyōshiki no chōshoku ga dekimasu ka

May I have some bread and coffee?

パンとコーヒーがほしいのですが

pan taw kaw-hee ga hosh-ee no dess ga

pan to kōhī ga hoshii no desu ga

May I have a boiled egg?

ゆで卵がほしいのですが

yoo-det-amago ga hosh-ee-no dess ga

yudetamago ga hoshii no desu ga

LIKELY REACTIONS

Have you an identity document, please?

身分証明書がありますか

mee-boon-shaw-may-shaw ga arry-mass ka

mibunshōmeisho ga arimasu ka

What's your name?
[see p. 19]

お名前は

onna-my wa

onamae wa

Sorry, we're full

すみませんが満員です

soo-mee-mass-en ga man-yeen dess

sumimasen ga man'in desu

I haven't any rooms left

部屋はありません

heyya wa arry-massen

heya wa arimasen

Do you want to have a look?　　ごらんになりますか
　　　　　　　　　　　　　　　go-ran nee narry-mass ka
　　　　　　　　　　　　　　　goran ni narimasu ka

How many people is it for?　　何名様ですか
　　　　　　　　　　　　　　　nan-mair-samma dess ka
　　　　　　　　　　　　　　　nanmeisama desu ka

From (7 o'clock) onward　　　（7時）からあと
　　　　　　　　　　　　　　　(sh-chee-jee) karra atto
　　　　　　　　　　　　　　　(shichi ji) kara ato

From (midday) onward　　　　（正午）から
[*For times, see p. 158*]　　　(shaw-gaw) karra
　　　　　　　　　　　　　　　(shōgo) kara

It's (5000) yen　　　　　　　（五千）円です
[*For numbers, see p. 154*]　　(gaw-sen) en dess
　　　　　　　　　　　　　　　(gosen) en desu

Camping and youth hostelling

ESSENTIAL INFORMATION
Camping

- Look for the words: キャンプ場 (campsite)
- There are not many places for camping in Japan. Those that exist are found on or near the beaches, mountain areas and in some public parks. Most campsites are open only in July and August.
- If you want further information on campsites check with the Japan Auto Camping Association.
- Beach bungalows バンガロー and mountain shacks 山小屋 are sometimes available and there are places where you can pitch a tent but always make sure it is permitted by inquiring first.

Youth hostels

- Look for the word: ユースホステル (youth hostel)
- Youth hostels are plentiful and a useful guide in English is published by the International Youth Hostel Federation (volume 2 includes Japan). There is also a free JNTO booklet *Youth Hostels in Japan.*
- There are many different types of youth hostel: public and private hostels, temples, shrines, private houses and ryokans. To stay at most youth hostels you will need a valid membership card.
- Generally little English is spoken.
- Advance booking is necessary.
- Finding a campsite and youth hostel, see p. 22.
- Replacing equipment, see p. 66.

WHAT TO SAY

I have a booking	予約してあります yoy-ak-oo shtay arry-mass yoyaku shite arimasu
Have you any vacancies?	あいていますか eye-tay-ee-mass ka aite imasu ka

It's for...
······です
...dess
...desu

one adult/one person
おとなひとり
o-tonna shtorry
otona hitori

two adults/two people
おとなふたり
o-tonna f-tarry
otona futari

and one child
とこどもひとり
toh kod-ommo shtorry
to kodomo hitori

and two children
とこどもふたり
toh kod-ommo f-tarry
to kodomo futari

It's for...
······です
...dess
...desu

one night
一泊
eep-pak-oo
ippaku

two nights
二泊
nee hak-oo
nihaku

one week
一週間
eesh-shoo-kan
isshūkan

two weeks
二週間
nee-shoo-kan
nishūkan

How much is it...
いくらですか
ee-koorra dess ka
ikura desu ka

for the tent?
テントは
ten-toh wa
tento wa

for the car?
車は
koo-roo-ma wa
kuruma wa

for the electricity?
電気代は
den-kee-dye wa
denkidai wa

per person?	ひとりあたり shtorry atta-ree hitori-atari
per day/night?	-泊/ -晩 eep-pak-oo/shtoh-ban ippaku/hitoban
May I look round?	見せてもらっていいですか mee-set-ay morrat-tay ee dess ka misete moratte ii desu ka
At what time do you lock up at night?	何時が門限ですか nan-jee ga mon-ghen dess ka nanji ga mongen desu ka
Do you provide anything...	……がありますか ...ga arry-mass ka ...ga arimasu ka
to eat?	食べもの tabbem-onno tabemono
to drink?	飲みもの nom-ee-monno nomimono
Do you have...	……がありますか ...ga arry-mass ka ...ga arimasu ka
a bar?	バー bar bā
hot showers?	お湯の出るシャワー o-yoo no derroo sha-wa oyu no deru shawā
a kitchen?	台所 dye-dokko-raw daidokoro
a launderette?	コインランドリー koyn land-oree koinrandorī
a restaurant?	食堂 shok-oo-daw shokudō
a shop?	店 mee-say mise

Do you have...

……がありますか

...ga arry-mass ka

...ga arimasu ka

a swimming pool?

プール

poo-loo

pūru

a snack-bar?

軽食堂

kay-shok-oo-daw

keishokudō

[*For food shopping, see p. 75, and for eating and drinking out, see p. 98*]

Where are...

……はどこですか

...wa dokko dess ka

...wa doko desu ka

the garbage cans?

ゴミ箱

gom-ee bak-aw

gomibako

the showers?

シャワー

sha-wah

shawā

the toilets?

トイレ

toy-ray

toire

At what time must one...

……は何時ですか

...wa nan-jee dess ka

...wa nanji desu ka

go to bed?

消灯

shaw-taw

shōtō

get up?

起床

kee-shaw

kishō

Please have you got...

……がありますか

...ga arry-mass ka

...ga arimasu ka

a broom?

ほうき

haw-kee

hōki

a corkscrew?

コルクぬき

korroo-koo noo-kee

korukunuki

a drying-up cloth?	布きん	
	f-keen	
	fukin	
a fork?	フォーク	
	faw-koo	
	fōku	
a fridge?	冷蔵庫	
	lay-zaw-kaw	
	reizōko	
a frying pan?	フライパン	
	fry-pan	
	furaipan	
an iron?	アイロン	
	eye-lon	
	airon	
a knife?	ナイフ	
	nye-foo	
	naifu	
a plate?	お皿	
	o-salla	
	osara	
a saucepan?	おなべ	
	o-nabbay	
	onabe	
a teaspoon?	おさじ	
	o-saj-ee	
	osaji	
a tin can opener?	カン切り	
	kan-kee-ree	
	kankiri	
any washing powder?	洗剤	
	sen-zye	
	senzai	
any washing-up liquid?	台所洗剤	
	dye dokko-raw sen-zye	
	daidokorosenzai	
The bill, please	いくらになりますか	
	ee-koorra nee narry-mass ka	
	ikura ni narimasu ka	

Problems

The toilet	トイレ toy-ray toire
The shower	シャワー sha-wa shawā
The tap	じゃぐち jag-oo-chee jaguchi
The razor point	電気カミソリ用のさしこみ den-kee kam-ee-sorry yaw no sash-ee-kom-ee denkikamisoriyō no sashikomi
The light	電気 den-kee denki
...is not working	……が故障しています ...ga kosh-aw shtay ee-mass ...ga koshō shite imasu
My camping gas has run out	キャンプ用のガスが切れました kee-amp-oo yaw no gass-oo ga kee-rem-ashta kyampuyō no gasu ga kiremashita

LIKELY REACTIONS

Have you an identity document?	身分証明書がありますか mee-boon-shaw-may shaw ga arry-mass ka mibunshōmeisho ga arimasu ka
Your membership card, please	会員カードを見せてください kye-een kah-doh o mee-set-tay koo-dass-eye kaiinkādo o misete kudasai
What's your name? [see p. 19]	お名前は onna-my wa onamae wa
Sorry, we're full	すみません、いっぱいです soo-mee-mass-en eep-pye dess sumimasen ippai desu

How many people is it for?	何名様ですか nan-mair-samma dess ka nanmeisama desu ka
How many nights is it for?	何泊ですか nam-pak-oo dess ka nanpaku desu ka
It's (2000) yen...	(二千) 円です (nee sen) en dess (ni sen)en desu
per day/per night [*For numbers, see p. 154*]	一泊/ 一晩 eep-pak-oo/shtoh-ban ippaku/hitoban

General shopping
The drugstore/The chemist's

ESSENTIAL INFORMATION

- Look for the words:
  くすり　　　(drug)
  薬局　　　(chemist's)
- Wherever you go pharmacists are competent in recommending effective drugs for common ailments which do not require a doctor's prescription.
- If you insist on imported medication you are likely to find these only in major metropolitan areas—hotels, department stores and drugstores.
- Other items are often sold, such as toilet articles and cosmetics, imported newspapers, pocketbooks and magazines but not film.
- Drugstores are open during normal business hours, i.e. from 9:00 a.m. to 6:30 p.m. including Sundays.
- Finding a drugstore, see p. 22.

WHAT TO SAY

I'd like...	……をください
	...oh koo-dass-eye
	...o kudasai
some Alka Seltzer	アルカセルツァー
	arroo-ka-serroo-tsah
	arukaserutsā
some antiseptic	消毒薬
	shaw-dokoo-ya-koo
	shōdokuyaku
some aspirin	アスピリン
	ass-pee-leen
	asupirin
some bandages	ほうたい
	haw-tie
	hōtai
some cotton wool	脱脂綿
	dash shim-en
	dasshimen

some cough drops	咳止め sek-ee-dom-ay sekidome
some eye drops	目薬 meghoo-soo-ree megusuri
some foot powder	足のパウダー ash-ee no pow-dah ashi no paudā
some gauze dressing	ガーゼ gah-zay gāze
some insect lotion	かゆみ止め ka-yoo-mee-dom-ay kayumidome
some insect repellent	殺虫剤 sat-choo-zye satchūzai
some lip salve	リップクリーム leep-poo-kleem-oo rippukurīmu
some nose drops	点鼻薬 tem-bee-ya-koo tenbiyaku
some sticking plaster	プラスター ばんそうこう poo-rass-tah/ban-saw-kaw purasutā/bansōkō
some throat lozenges	トローチ tollaw-chee torōchi
some Vaseline	ワセリン wassel-een waserin

I'd like something for...	……にきく薬がほしいんですが
	...nee kee-koo k-soo-ree ga
	  hosh-een dess ga
	...ni kiku kusuri ga hoshii n
	  desu ga

bites	かみ傷 ka-mee-kee-zoo kamikizu

I'd like something for...

······にきく薬がほしいんですが

...nee kee-koo k-soo-ree ga hosh-een dess ga

...ni kiku kusuri ga hoshii n desu ga

burns	やけど
	ya-keddo
	yakedo
car(air)/sea sickness	乗り物/船酔い
	norry-monno-yoy/foo-na-yoy
	norimono-yoi/funa-yoi
chilblains/frostbite	しもやけ
	shee-mow-ya-kay
	shimoyake
a cold	かぜ
	kazzay
	kaze
constipation	便秘
	bem-pee
	benpi
a cough	咳
	sek-ee
	seki
diarrhoea	下痢
	gherree
	geri
ear-ache	耳の痛み
	mee-mee no ee-tammy
	mimi no itami
flu	インフルエンザ
	een-floo-enzah
	infuruenza
scalds	やけど
	ya-keddo
	yakedo
sore gums	歯ぐきの痛み
	hag-oo-kee-no ee-tammy
	haguki no itami
sprains	ねんざ
	nenza
	nenza

stings (mosquito, bees)	虫さされ
	moo-shee-sa-sa-ray
	mushisasare
sunburn	日焼け
	hee-yakkay
	hiyake
I need...	……がほしいんですが
	...ga hosh-een dess ga
	...ga hoshii n desu ga
some baby food	ベビーフード
	bebby foo-daw
	bebī fūdo
some contraceptives	避妊薬
	hee-neen-yak-oo
	hininyaku
some deodorant	体臭止め
	tie-shoo-dom-ay
	taishūdome
some disposable diapers	使い捨てのおムツ
	t-sky-stay no om-oots-oo
	tsukaisute no omutsu
some handcream	ハンドクリーム
	han-daw koo-ree-moo
	hando kurīmu
some lipstick	口紅
	koo-chee benny
	kuchibeni
some make-up remover	化粧おとし
	kesh-aw ottosh-ee
	keshō otoshi
some paper tissues	ティッシュ
	teesh-shoo
	tisshu
some razor blades	カミソリ
	kammy-sorry
	kamisori
some safety pins	安全ピン
	anzen peen
	anzen pin
some sanitary napkins	生理用ナプキン
	say-ree-yaw nap-oo-keen
	seiriyō nappukin

I need...
……がほしいんですが
...ga hosh-een dess ga
...ga hoshii n desu ga

some shaving cream
ひげそり用クリーム
hee-ghess-orry yaw koo-ree-moo
higesoriyō kurīmu

some soap
せっけん
sek-ken
sekken

some suntan lotion/oil
サンタンローション/オイル
san-tan law-shon/oy-roo
santan rōshon/oiru

some talcum powder
タルカムパウダー
tal-kam pow-dah
tarukamu paudā

some tampons
タンポン
tam-pon
tanpon

some toilet paper
トイレットペーパー
toy-ret-toh pair-pah
toiretto pēpā

some toothpaste
歯みがき
[*For other essential
expressions, see 'Shop talk',
p. 69*]
hammy gakky
hamigaki

Holiday items

ESSENTIAL INFORMATION

- For almost any item your best bet is one of the large department stores. Some things are available at the resorts, such as beach parasols.
- For food, see picnic food p. 84.
- Film for prints is widely available (but not a very extensive selection) at ordinary shops, kiosks and department stores. Film for slides is not widely available.
- For getting film processed, look for this sign in Roman letters: **DPE** (Developing, Processing, Enlarging).
- In Tokyo the Shinjuku district is well known for camera equipment at bargain prices. Tourists can purchase cameras free of the national sales tax. However you will sometimes find that the discount offered by shops selling camera equipment with tax added to the prices can be greater than the 'bargain' at the tax-free shop.

WHAT TO SAY

Where can I buy...?	……はどこで買えますか
	...wa dokko dair ka-em-ass ka
	...wa doko de kaemasu ka
I'd like...	……がほしいのですが
	...ga hosh-ee no dess ga
	...ga hoshii no desu ga
a bag	バッグ
	bag-goo
	baggu
a beach ball	ビーチ・ボール
	bee-chee-baw-roo
	bīchibōru
a bucket	バケツ
	bakkets
	baketsu
an English newspaper	英字新聞
	ay-jee-shim-bun
	eijishimbun

I'd like...		……がほしいのですが
		...ga hosh-ee no dess ga
		...ga hoshii no desu ga
	some envelopes	封筒
		foo-taw
		fūtō
	a guide book	ガイドブック
		guy-doh book-koo
		gaidobukku
	a map (of the area)	(このあたりの) 地図
		(konno atta-ree no) chee-zoo
		(kono atari no) chizu
	some postcards	ハガキ
		hag-akky
		hagaki
	a spade	スコップ
		skop-poo
		sukoppu
	a straw hat	麦わら帽子
		moo-ghee-warra baw-shee
		mugiwarabōshi
	a suitcase	スーツケース
		soots-kairss
		sūtsukēsu
	some sunglasses	サングラス
		san goo-rass
		sangurasu
	a sunshade	日よけ
		hee-yokkay
		hiyoke
	an umbrella	かさ
		kassa
		kasa
	some writing paper	便せん
		been-sen
		binsen
I'd like... [*show the camera*]		……がほしいんですが
		...ga hosh-een dess ga
		...ga hoshii n desu ga
	a colour film	カラーフィルム
		karra fee-roo-moo
		karāfirumu

a black and white film	白黒フィルム
	shee-raw koo-raw fee-roo-moo
	shirokuro firumu
for prints	プリント
	poo-reen-toh
	purinto
for slides	スライド
	soo-rye-doh
	suraido
12(24/36) exposures	12 (24/36) 巻
	joo-nee (nee-joo-yon/san-joo-rok-oo) makky
	jūni (nijūyon/sanjūroku) maki
...please	……お願いします
	...on-eg-eye-shee-mass
	...onegai shimasu
a standard 8mm film	スタンダードの8ミリフィルム
	stan-dard-o no hatch-ee millee fee-roo-moo
	sutandādo no hachi miri firumu
a super 8 film	スーパー8
	soo-par airto
	sūpā ēto
some flash bulbs	フラッシュの玉
	fu-rash-oo no tamma
	furasshu no tama
This camera is broken	このカメラはこわれています
	konno kammerra wa ko-warret-ay-eemass
	kono kamera wa kowarete imasu
The film is stuck	フィルムがつまっています
	fee-roo-moo ga tsoo-mat-tay-eemass
	firumu ga tsumatte imasu
Please can you develop/print this?	これを現像/プリントしていただけますか
	korray o ghen-zaw/poo-reen-toh shtay ee-taddak-em-ass ka
	kore o genzō/purinto shite itadakemasu ka
Please can you load the camera?	フィルムをいれていただけますか
	fee-roo-moo o irret-ay ee-taddak em-ass ka
	firumu o irete itadakemasu ka

The following souvenir articles can be bought not only at speciality shops but at most of the numerous department stores:

cloisonné (enamel ware)	七宝焼
	sheep-paw-yak-ee
	shippōyaki
dolls	人形
	neeng-yaw
	ningyō
fans	扇子
	sen-soo
	sensu
folkcrafts	民芸品
	meen-gay-heen
	mingeihin
hanging-picture rolls	掛物
	kak-em-onno
	kakemono
kimono	着物
	kee-monno
	kimono
lacquerware	塗物
	noo-ree-monno
	nurimono
painted screens	屏風
	b-yaw-boo
	byōbu
paper products	紙製品
	kam-ee-say-heen
	kamiseihin
pearls	真珠
	sheen-joo
	shinju
pottery	陶磁器
	taw-jikky
	tōjiki
silks	絹
	kee-noo
	kinu
swords	刀剣類
	taw-ken-roo-ee
	tōkenrui
woodblock prints	木版画
[*For other essential expressions, see 'Shop talk' p. 69*]	mok-oo-hanga
	mokuhanga

The smoke shop

ESSENTIAL INFORMATION

- Look for this sign (almost anywhere): たばこ
- You usually get a free lighter if you buy several packets at one time.
- Imported cigarettes, cigars and pipe tobacco can usually only be found in hotels or department stores in metropolitan areas.
- Cigarettes can be bought at kiosks and from cigarette machines and inside coffee shops, snack bars, bars etc.
- To ask if there is a smoke shop near by, see p. 22.

WHAT TO SAY

A packet of cigarettes...	タバコを 一個……
	tabbak-aw o ik-kaw...
	tabako o ikko...
with filters	フィルター付きの
	feel-tart-skee
	firutātsuki no
without filters	フィルターなしの
	feel-ta nash-ee no
	firutānashi no
king size	キング・サイズの
	keen-g-size no
	kingu saizu no
menthol	メンソールの
	men-saw-roo no
	mensōru no
Those up there on the right	そこの右上の
	sokko no mee-ghee oo-ay no
	soko no migi ue no
Those up there on the left	そこの左上の
	sokko no hee-da-ree oo-ay no
	soko no hidari ue no
These [*point*]	これ
	korray
	kore
Cigarettes, please	タバコをください
	tabbak-aw o koo-dass-eye
	tabako o kudsai

Two packets
二個
nee-kaw
niko

Have you got...
……がありますか
...ga arry-mass ka
...ga arimasu ka

English cigarettes?
英国のタバコ
ay-kok-oo no tabbak-aw
eikoku no tabako

American cigarettes?
アメリカのタバコ
am-ellee-ka no tabbak-aw
amerika no tabako

English pipe tobacco?
イギリスのパイプタバコ
ee-ghee-reess no pye-poo
  tabbak-aw
igirisu no paipu tabako

American pipe tobacco?
アメリカのパイプタバコ
am-ellee-ka no pye-poo
  tabbak-aw
amerika no paipu tabako

rolling tobacco?
巻きタバコ
makkee tabbak-aw
makitabako

That one down there on the
  right
そこの右下の
sokko no mee-ghee sh-ta no
soko no migi shita no

That one down there on the
  left
そこの左下の
sokko no hee-da-ree sh-ta no
soko no hidari shita no

This one [*point*]
これ
korray
kore

A cigar, please
葉巻を一本ください
ham-ak-ee-o eep-pon koo-dass-eye
hamaki o ippon kudasai

That one [*point*]
それ
sorray
sore

Some cigars, please
葉巻をください
ham-ak-ee o koo-dass-eye
hamaki o kudasai

Those [*point*]	それ sorray sore
A box of matches	マッチを 一箱 matchee o sh-toh hak-aw matchi o hitohako
A packet of pipe-cleaners	パイプクリーナーを 一箱 pye-poo koo-ree-nah o sh-toh hak-aw paipu kurīnā o hitohako
A packet of flints [*show lighter*]	ライターの石を 一箱 lie-tar no ish-ee o sh-toh hak-aw raitā no ishi o hitohako
Lighter fluid	ライターのガス lie-tar no gass raitā no gasu
Lighter gas, please	ライターのガスをください lie-tar no gass-o koo-dass-eye raitā no gasu o kudasai

[*For other essential expressions, see 'Shop talk', p. 69*]

Buying clothes

ESSENTIAL INFORMATION

- Look for:
  婦人服 (women's clothes)
  紳士服 (men's clothes)
  靴店 (shoe shop)
- It is sometimes difficult to find ready-made clothes for larger framed people.
- Any number of small shops and department stores make tailor-made clothing but these are very expensive.
- Enough English is generally understood/spoken at the department stores for basic communication but not in smaller shops unless you're lucky.
- Don't buy without being measured first or without trying things on.
- Don't rely on conversion charts of clothing sizes.
- If you are buying for someone else, take their measurements with you (in centimetres).

WHAT TO SAY

I'd like...	……がほしいんですが
	...ga hosh-een dess ga
	...ga hoshii n desu ga
an anorak/parka	アノラック
	anno-rak-koo
	anorakku
a belt	ベルト
	bel-toh
	beruto
a bikini	ビキニ
	bee-kee-nee
	bikini
a bra	ブラジャー
	boo-raj-yah
	burajyā
a cap (swimming)	水泳帽
	soo-ee-air-baw
	suieibō

a cap (skiing)	スキー帽
	skee-baw
	sukībō
a cardigan	カーディガン
	kah-dee-gan
	kādigan
a coat	コート
	kaw-toh
	kōto
a dress	ドレス
	dorress
	doresu
a hat	帽子
	baw-shee
	bōshi
a jacket	上着
	oo-waggy
	uwagi
a jumper	ジャンパー
	jam-pa
	janpā
a pullover	プルオーバー
	poo-roo-oba
	puruōbā
a nightdress	ねまき
	nem-ak-ee
	nemaki
some pyjamas	パジャマ
	paj-amma
	pajama
a raincoat	レインコート
	lay-n-kaw-toh
	reinkōto
a shirt (women)	ブラウス シャツ
	boo-lowss/shats
	burausu/shatsu
a shirt (men)	シャツ ワイシャツ
	shats/wye-shats
	shatsu/waishatsu
a skirt	スカート
	skah-toh
	sukāto

I'd like... ……がほしいんですが
...ga hosh-een dess ga
...ga hoshii n desu ga

a suit スーツ
soots
sūtsu

a swimsuit 水着
mee-zoo-ghee
mizugi

some tights タイツ
tights
taitsu

some trousers ズボン
z-bon
zubon

a T-shirt Tシャツ
tee shats
tīshatsu

a pair of briefs (women) パンティ
panty
pantī

a pair of gloves 手袋
teb-ookoo-raw
tebukuro

a pair of jeans ジーンズ
jeans
jīnzu

a pair of shorts ショーツ
shorts
shōtsu

a pair of (long/short) socks (長い/短い)くつ下
(mee-jee-kye/nag-eye)k-tsoo-sh-ta
(mijikai/nagai)kutsushita

a pair of stockings ストッキング
stok-ing-goo
sutokkingu

a pair of underpants (men) パンツ
pants
pantsu

I'd like a pair of... ……が一足ほしいんですが
...ga iss-sokkoo hosh-een dess ga
...ga issoku hoshii n desu ga

shoes	くつ
	k-tsoo
	kutsu
canvas shoes	布ぐつ
	noo-no-g-tsoo
	nunogutsu
sandals	サンダル
	san-darroo
	sandaru
beach shoes	ビーチシューズ
	beech-shoo-zoo
	bīchishūzu
boots	ブーツ
	boots
	būtsu
moccasins	モカシン
	mokka-sheen
	mokashin
My size is...	私のサイズは……
[*For numbers, see p. 154*]	wattash-ee no sye-zoo wa...
	watashi no saizu wa...
Can you measure me, please?	サイズをはかってくださいますか
	sye-zoo o hakkat tekkoo-dass-eye mass ka
	saizu o hakatte kudasai-masu ka
Can I try it on?	試着していいですか
	sh-cha-koo sh-tay-ee dess ka
	shichaku shite ii desu ka
It's for a present	贈り物にするんです
	o-koo-ree-monno nee soo-roon dess
	okurimono ni suru n desu
These are the measurements	これがサイズです
[*show written*]	korray ga sighs dess
	kore ga saizu desu
bust	バスト
	ba-stoh
	basuto
chest	胸回り
	moo-nemma-warry
	munemawari
collar	えり
	erry
	eri

These are the measurements [*show written*]	これがサイズです korray ga sighs dess kore ga saizu desu
hip	ヒップ hip-poo hippu
leg	足 ash-ee ashi
waist	ウエスト wair-sto uesuto

Have you got something...

	……がありますか ...ga arry-mass ka ...ga arimasu ka
in black?	黒いの koo-roy no kuroi no
in white?	 shee-roy no shiroi no
in gray?	グレーの goo-rair no gurē no
in blue?	青いの ah-oy no aoi no
in brown?	茶色の cha-ee-raw no chairo no
in pink?	ピンクの peenk no pinku no
in green?	緑色の mee-dorree-ee-raw no midoriiro no
in red?	赤の akka no aka no
in yellow?	黄色の kee-ee-raw no kiiro no

in this colour? [*point*]	この色の
	konno ee-raw no
	kono iro no
in cotton?	木綿の
	mom-en no
	momen no
in denim?	デニムの
	den-eem no
	denimu no
in leather?	皮の
	ka-wa no
	kawa no
in nylon?	ナイロンの
	nye-ee-ron no
	nairon no
in suede?	スウェードの
	swair-doh no
	suwēdo no
in wool?	ウールの
	ooroo no
	ūru no
in this material? [*point*]	この素材の
	konno soz-eye no
	kono sozai no

[*For other essential expressions, see 'Shop talk', p. 69*]

Replacing equipment

ESSENTIAL INFORMATION

- Look for these shops and signs:
  - 金物 (hardware)
  - 家庭用品 (household goods)
  - 電気器具 (electrical goods)
  - 台所用品 (household cleaning materials)
- There are numerous hardware stores, bag and luggage shops, electrical appliance shops, etc. and department stores which are well stocked.
- In Tokyo the Akihabara district is well known for domestic electrical goods at bargain prices. To get there, take the yellow Sobu (saw-boo) line.
- To ask the way to the shop, see p. 22.

WHAT TO SAY

Have you got...	……がありますか
	...ga arry-mass ka
	...ga arimasu ka
an adaptor? [*show appliance*]	アダプター
	addap-tah
	adaputā
a bottle of butane gas?	ブタンガス
	boo-tan gass
	butangasu
a bottle of propane gas?	プロパンガス
	poo-roppan gass
	puropan gasu
a bottle opener?	栓抜き
	sen-noo-kee
	sennuki
a corkscrew?	コルク抜き
	koroo-koo noo-kee
	korukunuki
any disinfectant?	消毒剤
	shaw-dok-oo zye
	shōdokuzai

any disposable cups?	使い捨てのコップ
	t-sky-stay no kop-poo
	tsukaisute no koppu
any disposable plates?	使い捨てのお皿
	t-sky-stay no o-salla
	tsukaisute no osara
a drying-up cloth?	布きん
	f-keen
	fukin
any forks?	フォーク
	fork-oo
	fōku
a fuse? [*show old one*]	ヒューズ
	hughes
	fyūzu
an insecticide spray?	殺虫スプレー
	sat-choo sprair
	satchū supurē
a paper kitchen roll?	ペーパータオル
	pair-pah ta-wor-oo
	pēpā taoru
any knives?	ナイフ
	nye-foo
	naifu
a light bulb? [*show old one*]	電球
	denk-yoo
	denkyū
a plastic bucket?	プラスチック・バケツ
	poo-rass-chick bakkets
	purasuchikku baketsu
a plastic can?	プラスチック・カン
	poo-rass-chick kan
	purasuchikku kan
a scouring pad?	なべみがき
	nabbay-mee-gak-ee
	nabemigaki
a spanner/wrench?	スパナ
	spanna
	supana
a sponge?	スポンジ
	spon-jee
	suponji

Have you got... ······がありますか
...ga arry-mass ka
...ga arimasu ka

any string? ひも
hee-mo
himo

any tent pegs? テント用のくい
ten-toh yaw-no-kwee
tentoyō no kui

a tin can opener? カン切り
kan kee-ree
kankiri

a flashlight? 懐中電灯
kye-choo-den-taw
kaichūdentō

any flashlight batteries? 電池
den-chee
denchi

a universal plug (for the sink)? プラグ
poo-rag-goo
puragu

a clothesline? ものほしロープ
monno-hosh-ee raw-poo
monohoshirōpu

any laundry detergent? 洗剤
sen-zye
senzai

a scrubbing brush? タワシ
ta-wa-shee
tawashi

any dishwashing liquid? 台所用洗剤
dye-dokko-raw-yaw-sen-zye
daidokoroyōsenzai

[*For other essential expressions, see 'Shop talk', p. 69*]

Shop talk

ESSENTIAL INFORMATION

- Don't be surprised if the shop assistants all shout いらっしゃいませ (irrash-eye-mass-air/irrasshaimase) 'welcome' when you enter the shop and ありがとうございました (arry-gattaw goz-eye-mash-ta/arigatō gozaimashita) 'thank you very much'. It's all part of the service in Japan.
- English and other foreign languages are not generally understood or spoken in shops but sign language, or, especially, writing things down (in English) usually gets you through.
- Many shops are open on Sundays closing one day mid-week instead.
- It is helpful if you know a few essential expressions such as 'how much'. You should also know your coins and notes:
  coins: see illustration overleaf.
  notes: 1000, 5000, 10000 yen.
- Know how to say the important weights and measures:

50 grams	50グラム gaw-joo goo-ram-oo gojū guramu
100 grams	100グラム h-yak-oo goo-ram-oo hyaku guramu
200 grams	200グラム nee h-yak-oo goo-ram-oo nihyaku guramu
½ kilo	¥キロ han-kee-law hankiro
1 kilo	1キロ ee-chee kee-law ichi kiro
2 kilos	2キロ nee kee-law ni kiro
½ litre	¥リットル han leet-torroo han rittoru

1 litre	1リットル ee-chee leet-torroo ichi rittoru
2 litres [*For numbers, see p. 154*]	2リットル nee leet-torroo ni rittoru

CUSTOMER

I'm just looking	見せてもらっているところです mee-set-ay morrat-tay-ee-roo tokko-raw dess misete moratte iru tokoro desu
Excuse me	すみません soo-mee-mass-en sumimasen
How much is this/that?	これ/それはいくらですか korray/sorray wa ee-koorra dess ka kore/sore wa ikura desu ka
What is that/are those?	あれはなんですか array wa nan-dess ka are wa nan desu ka
Is there a discount?	割引きはありますか wa-ree-bee-kee wa arry-mass ka waribiki wa arimasu ka
I'd like that, please	それをください sorray o koo-dass-eye sore o kudasai
I won't take it, thank you	けっこうです kek-kaw dess kekkō desu
Not that	それじゃありません sorray ja arry-mass-en sore ja arimasen
Something like this/that	こう, そういうのです kaw/saw-yoo no dess kō/sō iu no desu
That's enough, thank you	それでじゅうぶんです. ありがとう sorred-air joo-bun dess arry-gattaw sore de jūbun desu.arigatō

More please	もっとお願いします mot-taw o-neg-eye-shee-mass motto onegai shimasu

Less please	もうすこし少なくしてください
	maw skosh-ee skoo-nak-shtay
	   koo-dass-eye
	mō sukoshi sukunaku shite
	   kudasai

That's fine/OK	いいです ee dess ii desu
I'll take it with me	持ってかえります mot-tay kye-ree-mass motte kaerimasu
Please send it to this address	この住所に送ってください konno joo-shaw nee okoot-tay koo-dass-eye kono jūsho ni okutte kudasai
There won't be any difficulty with the customs, will there?	税関で問題はないでしょうね zay-kan-dair mon-dye wa nye deshaw nair zeikan de mondai wa nai deshō ne
It's not right	ちがっています ching-at-tay-ee-mass chigatte imasu
Thank you very much	どうもありがとう daw-maw arry-gattaw dōmo arigatō
Have you got something...	……はありませんか ...wa arry-mass-en ka ...wa arimasen ka
better?	もっといいの mot-taw ee no motto ii no
cheaper?	もっと安いの mot-taw yass-ee no motto yasui no
different?	ちがうの ching-ow no chigau no

larger?	もっと大きいの mot-taw aw-kee no motto ōkii no
smaller?	もっと小さいの mot-taw chee-sye no motto chiisai no
At what time...	何時に…… nan-jee nee nanji ni...
do you open?	あきますか ak-ee-mass ka akimasu ka
do you close?	しまりますか shee-ma-ree-mass ka shimarimasu ka
Can I have a bag, please?	袋をいただけますか f-koo-raw o ee-taddak-em-ass ka fukuro o itadakemasu ka
Can I have a receipt?	レシートをいただけますか lesh-eet-o o ee-taddak-em-ass ka reshīto o itadakemasu ka
Do you take...	……でいいですか ...day ee dess ka ...de ii desu ka
dollars/pounds?	ドル/ポンド dorroo/pondo doru/pondo
traveler's checks?	トラベラーズ・チェック tol-ab-ellarz chek-koo toraberāzu chekku
credit cards?	クレジットカード koo-rej-eet-toh kah-doh kurejitto kādo
I'd like...	……ほしいんですが ...hosh-een dess ga ...hoshii n desu ga
one like that	そういうのをひとつ saw-yoo no o shtots sō iu no o hitotsu
two like that	そういうのをふたつ saw-yoo no o f-tats sō iu no o futatsu

SHOP ASSISTANT

Can I help you?	なにをさしあげましょうか
	nannee o sash-ee-ag-em-ash-aw ka
	nani o sashiagemashō ka
What would you like?	なにをおさがしですか
	nannee o sag-ash-ee dess ka
	nani o osagashi desu ka
Will that be all?	それでぜんぶですか
	sorray dez-en-boo dess ka
	sore de zenbu desu ka
Anything else?	ほかになにか
	hok-an-ee-na nee ka
	hoka ni nani ka
Will you take it with you or shall we send it?	お持ち帰りになりますか、 それともお届けしましょうか
	o-motch-ee kye-ree nee-narry-mass ka sorret-ommo toddo-kesh-ee-mash-aw ka
	omochikaeri ni narimasu ka. soretomo otodoke shimashō ka
Sorry, none left	すみません、売り切れです
	soo-mee-mass-en oo-ree-kee-red-ess
	sumimasen. urikire desu
I haven't got any	おいてないんです
	oy-tay nine dess
	oite nai n desu
I haven't got any more	もうないんです
	maw nine dess
	mō nai n desu
How many do you want?	いくつさしあげましょうか
	ee-koot-soo sash-ee-ag-em-ash-aw ka
	ikutsu sashiagemashō ka
How much do you want?	どのぐらいさしあげましょうか
	donno goo-rye sash-ee-ag-em-ash-aw ka
	dono gurai sashiagemashō ka
Is that enough?	これでいいですか
	korray day ee dess ka
	kore de ii desu ka

Shopping for food
Bread

ESSENTIAL INFORMATION

- Finding a baker's, see p. 22.
- Key word to look for: パン (bread)
- Supermarkets of any size and general stores nearly always sell bread.
- The Japanese have a very limited variety of their own breads (usually white dough, sometimes filled with sweet bean paste or minced pork and vegetables).
- Brown breads are not available except at delicatessens and foreign food speciality shops in large cities.

WHAT TO SAY

Some bread, please	パンをください pan o koo-dass-eye pan o kudasai
A large loaf	大きいパン aw-kee pan ōkii pan
A small loaf	小さいパン chee-sye pan chiisai pan
A bread roll	ロール raw-loo rōru
Sliced bread	スライス soo-lie-soo suraisu
White bread	白いパン shee-roy pan shiroi pan
Rye bread	ライ麦パン lie moo-ghee pan raimugi pan

Wholemeal bread	ホールミールパン
	haw-roo-mee-roo pan
	hōrumīru pan
Two loaves	パンふたつ
	pan f-tats
	pan futatsu
Four bread rolls	ロールを四つ
	raw-loo o yot-soo
	rōru o yottsu

Cakes

ESSENTIAL INFORMATION

● Key words to look for:
   パンとケーキ (bread and cake shop)
   洋菓子　　　(cake shop)
● To find a cake shop, see p. 22.
● A wide range of traditional cakes and other sweets can be found in small shops all over the country and also in department stores.
● Western-style cakes are sold extensively and coffee shops serve them, too.
● In either case less butter or margarine is used in the baking and for the icing so they do not taste as 'rich' as American cakes. Typical Western treats such as doughnuts are less commonly found.

WHAT TO SAY

カステラ	
kass-tella	sponge cake
kasutera	
ドーナツ	
daw-nats	doughnut
dōnatsu	
チーズケーキ	
cheez-kair-kee	cheesecake
chīzukēki	

チョコレートケーキ
chokko-lair-tok-air-kee
chokorēto kēki   chocolate cake

アップルパイ
ap-poo-roo-pye   apple pie
appuru pai

ババロア
babba-loo-ah   Bavaroise
babaroa

ショートケーキ
shaw-tok-air-kee   fresh cream on a sponge base
shōto kēki   decorated with strawberries

エクレア
ek-lay-ah   a cream puff covered with
ekureā   chocolate

シュークリーム
shoo-klee-moo   a cream puff
shūkurīmu

せんべい
sen-bay   a rice cracker
senbei

ようかん
yaw-kan   sweet aduki beans paste
yōkan

くずもち
koo-zoo-motch-ee   a cake made from arrowroot
kuzumochi   starch (kudzu) served with soya
まんじゅう   bean powder and molasses
man-jew   steamed rice sponge cake with
manjū   sweet bean paste in the centre

You usually buy individual pastries by number:

Can I have this one please?   これください
                                     korray koo-dass-eye
                                     kore kudasai
Two pieces of this one,   これをふたつください
  please   **korray o f-tats koo-dass-eye**
                                     kore o futatsu kudasai

Ice cream and sweets

ESSENTIAL INFORMATION

● Key words to look for:
アイスクリーム (ice cream)
甘味処 (sweet shop)
洋菓子 (cake shop)
● Variety is limited but there are some multi-flavour ice cream parlours in big cities. Chocolate syrups are usually the only toppings available.
● Some US/European ice creams are made locally under licence.
● There is a wide variety of Japanese sweets which are particularly good with green tea.
● Pre-packed sweets are available in general stores and supermarkets.
● There are many ice cream stalls and mobile vendors in the summer.
● Soft ice cream ソフトクリーム (sof-tok-lee-moo/sofutokurīmu) is a particular favourite.

WHAT TO SAY

A...ice cream, please	……アイスクリームください
	...eye-ss-koo-ree-moo koo-dass-eye
	...aisukurīmu kudasai
strawberry	ストロベリー
	storraw-belly
	sutoroberī
chocolate	チョコレート
	chokko-rair-toh
	chokorēto
vanilla	バニラ
	ban-eella
	banira
matcha (green tea)	抹茶
	match-ah
	matcha
lemon	レモン
	lem-on
	remon

A waffle, please	ワッフルください
	waff-foo-roo koo-dass-eye
	waffuru kudasai

Over the counter

A single portion	シングル
	sheen-goo-roo
	shinguru
Two single portions	シングルふたつ
	sheen-goo-roo f-tats
	shinguru futatsu
A double portion	ダブル
	dabboo-roo
	daburu
Two double portions	ダブルふたつ
	dabboo-roo f-tats
	daburu futatsu
A cone	コーン
	korn
	kōn
A tub	カップ
	kap-poo
	kappu
A popsicle	棒付きアイス
	bawt-skee eye-ss
	bōtsuki aisu

At the sweet shop

Can I have a packet of...	……を一袋ください
	...o shtoh hoo-koo-ro koo-dass-eye
	...o hitofukuro kudasai
100 grams of...	……を100グラム
	...o h-yak-oo goo-ram-oo
	...o hyaku guramu
200 grams of...	……を200グラム
	...o nee h-yak-oo goo-ram-oo
	...o nihyaku guramu
sweets	キャンディー あめ
	kee-an-dee/am-ay
	kyandī/ame
chocolates	チョコレート
	chokko-rair-toh
	chokorēto

cookies	クッキー
	kook-kee
	kukkī
A box of...	……を 一箱
	...o shtoh hak-aw
	...o hitohako
Give me 100 grams of these and 200 grams of those	これを100グラムとあれを200グラムください
	korray o h-yak-oo goo-ram-oo toh array o nee h-yak-oo goo-ram-oo koo-dass-eye
	kore o hyaku guramu to are o nihyaku guramu kudasai
No, not those... [*point*]	それじゃありません
	sorray ja arry-mass-en
	sore ja arimasen
those	それです
	sorray dess
	sore desu
to the left	左のです
	hee-da-ree-no dess
	hidari no desu
to the right	右のです
	mee-ghee-no dess
	migi no desu
above	上のです
	oo-ay-no dess
	ue no desu
below	下のです
	shta-no dess
	shita no desu

[*For other essential expressions, see 'Shop talk', p. 69*]

In the supermarket

ESSENTIAL INFORMATION

- The place to look for:
  - スーパー (supermarket)
  - 食料品店 (general food store)
- Key instructions on signs in the shop:
  - 入口 (entrance)
  - 出口 (exit)
  - 会計 (check-out, cash desk)
  - サービス (on offer)
  - 特別サービス (special offer)
  - セルフサービス (self-service)
- There are many large chain-store supermarkets around and almost all department stores have a very extensive range of foods (usually in the basement).
- Opening times vary but most shops are open between 8:00 a.m. and 7:00 p.m.
- Supermarkets and department stores are usually open all day Sunday and some small stores stay open 24 hours.
- No need to say anything in a supermarket, but ask if you can't see what you want.
- For non-food items, see 'Replacing equipment', p. 66.

WHAT TO SAY

Excuse me, please	すみませんが
	soo-mee-mass-en-ga
	sumimasen ga
Where is...	……はどこですか
	...wa dokko dess ka
	...wa doko desu ka
the bread?	パン
	pan
	pan
the butter?	バター
	battah
	batā
the cheese?	チーズ
	cheez-oo
	chīzu

Where is...　　　　　　　　　　……はどこですか
　　　　　　　　　　　　　　　　...wa dokko dess ka
　　　　　　　　　　　　　　　　...wa doko desu ka

　　the chocolate?　　　　　　　チョコレート
　　　　　　　　　　　　　　　　chokko-rair-toh
　　　　　　　　　　　　　　　　chokoreto

　　the coffee?　　　　　　　　　コーヒー
　　　　　　　　　　　　　　　　kaw-hee
　　　　　　　　　　　　　　　　kōhī

　　the cooking oil?　　　　　　　調理用油
　　　　　　　　　　　　　　　　chaw-ree-yaw ab-oo-ra
　　　　　　　　　　　　　　　　chōriyō abura

　　the fresh fish section?　　　　鮮魚コーナー
　　　　　　　　　　　　　　　　seng-yaw korn-ah
　　　　　　　　　　　　　　　　sengyo kōnā

　　the fruit?　　　　　　　　　　くだもの
　　　　　　　　　　　　　　　　koo-da-monno
　　　　　　　　　　　　　　　　kudamono

　　the jam?　　　　　　　　　　ジャム
　　　　　　　　　　　　　　　　jam-oo
　　　　　　　　　　　　　　　　jamu

　　the meat?　　　　　　　　　　肉
　　　　　　　　　　　　　　　　nee-koo
　　　　　　　　　　　　　　　　niku

　　the milk?　　　　　　　　　　牛乳
　　　　　　　　　　　　　　　　ghee-oo-new
　　　　　　　　　　　　　　　　gyūnyū

　　the salt?　　　　　　　　　　塩
　　　　　　　　　　　　　　　　shee-aw
　　　　　　　　　　　　　　　　shio

　　the sugar?　　　　　　　　　砂糖
　　　　　　　　　　　　　　　　sat-aw
　　　　　　　　　　　　　　　　satō

　　the tea (English)?　　　　　　紅茶
　　　　　　　　　　　　　　　　kaw-cha
　　　　　　　　　　　　　　　　kōcha

　　the tea (Japanese)?　　　　　お茶
　　　　　　　　　　　　　　　　o-cha
　　　　　　　　　　　　　　　　ocha

　　the vegetable section?　　　　野菜のコーナー
　　　　　　　　　　　　　　　　yass-eye no korn-ah
　　　　　　　　　　　　　　　　yasai no kōnā

the vinegar?	酢
	soo
	su
the wine?	ワイン
	wye-een
	wain
the yoghurt?	ヨーグルト
	yaw-goo-roo-toh
	yōguruto
Where are...	……はどこですか
	...wa dokko dess ka
	...wa doko desu ka
the biscuits?	ビスケット
	bees-ket-toh
	bisuketto
the chips?	ポテト・チップス
	pot-etto cheep-soo
	poteto chippusu
the eggs?	卵
	tam-aggo
	tamago
the frozen foods?	冷凍食品
	lay-tor shok-oo heen
	reitōshokuhin
the fruit juices?	フルーツ・ジュース
	f-roots jooss
	furūtsu jūsu
the pastas?	めん類
	men-roo-ee
	menrui
the soft drinks?	ソフト・ドリンク
	soft-o dor-een-koo
	sofuto dorinku
the sweets?	お菓子
	o-kash-ee
	okashi
the canned vegetables?	野菜のカン詰め
	yass-eye no kan-zoo-may
	yasai no kanzume
the canned foods?	カン詰め
	kan-zoo-may
	kanzume

[*For other essential expressions, see 'Shop talk', p. 69*]

Picnic food

ESSENTIAL INFORMATION

- Key words to look for:
  お惣菜 (delicatessen)
  お弁当 (lunch box, ben-taw/bentō)
- Japanese picnic food お弁当 (ben-taw/bentō) is on sale at small grocers' shops, railway platform kiosks and in the basements of department stores.
- Ekiben is a particular type of lunch box only available on trains or at railway stations.
- You will also usually find that sandwiches and food is available at small stands in beach or mountain resorts.
- Weight guide:
  4–6 oz/150 g of prepared salad per two people, if eaten as a starter to a substantial meal.
  3–4 oz/100 g of prepared salad per person, if to be eaten as the main part of a picnic-type meal.

WHAT TO SAY

Can I have...	……をください
	...o koo-dass-eye
	...o kudasai
cheese sandwiches	チーズサンドイッチ
	cheez sando-ee-chee
	chīzu sandoitchi
egg sandwiches	エッグサンドイッチ
	eg-goo sando-ee-chee
	eggu sandoitchi
tuna sandwiches	ツナサンドイッチ
	ts-oonna sando-ee-chee
	tsuna sandoitchi
mixed sandwiches	ミックスサンドイッチ
	meek-soo sando-ee-chee
	mikkusu sandoitchi
100 grams of...	……を100グラム
	...o h-yak-oo goo-ram-oo
	...o hyaku guramu

150 grams of...	……を150グラム ...o h-yak-oo go-joo goo-ram-oo ...o hyaku gojū guramu
200 grams of...	……を200グラム ...o nee h-yak-oo goo-ram-oo ...o nihyaku guramu
300 grams of...	……を300グラム o sanb-yak-oo goo-ram-oo ...o sambyaku guramu
potato salad	ポテトサラダ pot-etto sal-adda poteto sarada
vegetable salad	野菜サラダ yass-eye sal-adda yasai sarada
cooked ham	ハム ham-oo hamu
this/that [*point*]	これ それ korray/sorray kore/sore

You might also like to try some of these:

お弁当 ben-taw bentō	lunch box
いなりずし ee-narry-zoo-shee inarizushi	seasoned rice stuffed into a bag of fried Tofu (bean curd)
太巻き f-tom-ak-ee futomaki	seasoned rice wrapped in seaweed, egg, vegetables and other ingredients
すし soo-shee sushi	seasoned rice balls with raw fish; a very popular dish with many varieties (see below)
ちらしずし chee-rash-ee zoo-shee chirashizushi	seasoned rice covered with cooked or marinated fish
押しずし osh-ee zoo-shee oshizushi	pressed seasoned rice with cooked fish on top and cut into squares (most sushi is eaten with your fingers)

釜めし kammo-mesh-ee kamameshi	seasoned rice with a lot of cooked vegetables on top, served in a kama bowl
おにぎり o-neeghee-ree onigiri	rice balls wrapped in seaweed
さけ sak-ay sake	rice balls with salmon in the centres
梅ぼし oo-mebbosh-ee umeboshi	rice balls with salted plums in the centres
たらこ tarrak-o tarako	rice balls with fish roe in the centres
春巻き harroo-mak-ee harumaki	spring rolls
しゅうまい shoo-mye shūmai	steamed pork meat balls wrapped in a thin pastry
ぎょうざ ghee-aw-za gyōza	crescent shaped pastries stuffed with chives and pork
かまぼこ kam-ab-okko kamaboko	boiled fish paste
ちくわ chee-koo-wa chikuwa	a kind of fish paste
コロノケ korrok-kay korokke	a croquette (potato)
つけもの ts-kem-onno tsukemono	pickled (salted) vegetables

[*For other essential expressions, see 'Shop talk', p. 69*]

Fruit and vegetables

ESSENTIAL INFORMATION

- Key words to look for:
  果物 (fruit)
  野菜 (vegetables)
  八百屋 (greengrocer)
- Most Japanese peel their fruit as these are usually heavily treated with chemicals.
- Fruit is generally larger than its European or American counter-part.
- Weight guide: 1 kg of potatoes is sufficient for six people for one meal.

WHAT TO SAY

½ kilo of...	······を500グラム ...o gaw h-yak-oo goo-ram-oo ...o gohyaku guramu
1 kilo of...	······を1キロ ...o ee-chee kee-law ...o ichi kiro
2 kilos of...	······を2キロ ...o nee kee-law ...o ni kiro
apples	りんご leen-gaw ringo
bananas	バナナ ban-anna banana
cherries	さくらんぼ sak-oo-ran-baw sakurambo
grapes	ぶどう boo-daw budō
oranges	オレンジ or-en-jee orenji

1 kilo of...	……を1キロ	
	...o ee-chee kee-law	
	...o ichi kiro	
peaches	桃	
	mommo	
	momo	
pears	なし	
	nash-ee	
	nashi	
plums	梅	
	oo-may	
	ume	
strawberries	いちご	
	ee-chee-gaw	
	ichigo	
tangerines	みかん	
	mee-kan	
	mikan	
A pineapple, please	パイナップルください	
	pie-nap-oo-loo koo-dass-eye	
	painappuru kudasai	
A grapefruit	グレープフルーツ	
	goo-rair-poo-foo-roots	
	gurēpufurūtsu	
A melon	メロン	
	mel-on	
	meron	
A water melon	すいか	
	see-ka	
	suika	
½ kilo of...	……を500グラム	
	...o gaw h-yak-oo goo-ram-oo	
	...o gohyaku guramu	
1 kilo of...	……を1キロ	
	...o ee-chee kee-law	
	...o ichi kiro	
2 kilos of...	……を2キロ	
	...o mee kee-law	
	...o ni kiro	
aubergines/eggplant	なす	
	nass-oo	
	nasu	

avocado pears	アボカド	
	ab-aw kaddaw	
	abokado	
carrots	にんじん	
	neen-jeen	
	ninjin	
corn on the cob	とうもろこし	
	taw-morro-kosh-ee	
	tōmorokoshi	
green beans	さやいんげん	
	sa-ya-een-ghen	
	sayaingen	
green peppers	ピーマン	
	pee-man	
	pīman	
mushrooms	マッシュルーム	
	mash-loom-oo	
	masshurūmu	
onions	たまねぎ	
	tam-an-eg-ee	
	tamanegi	
potatoes	じゃがいも	
	jag-eye-maw	
	jagaimo	
pumpkins	かぼちゃ	
	kabbo-cha	
	kabocha	
red cabbage	赤キャベツ	
	ak-ak-yabbets	
	akakyabetsu	
spinach	ほうれんそう	
	haw-ren-saw	
	hōrensō	
sprouts	芽キャベツ	
	mek-yabbets	
	mekyabetsu	
tomatoes	トマト	
	tom-attoh	
	tomato	

A bunch of...
......を 一束
...o shtoh tabba
...o hitotaba

  celery
セロリ
sel-ol-ee
serori

  parsley
パセリ
pass-el-ee
paseri

A head of garlic
にんにく
neen-nee-koo
ninniku

lettuce
レタス
let-ass
retasu

A cauliflower
カリフラワー
kal-ee-fra-wa
karifurawā

A cabbage
キャベツ
kee-abbets
kyabetsu

A cucumber
きゅうり
kew-ree
kyūri

Like that, please
それください
sorray koo-dass-eye
sore kudasai

Here are some fruit and vegetables which may not be familiar:

かき
kak-ee
kaki
persimmon

いちじく
ee-chee-jee-koo
ichijiku
fig

夏みかん
nats-oo-mee-kan
natsumikan
summer orange

なし
nash-ee
nashi
a type of pear which looks like an apple but which is rather hard and watery

大根 dye-kon **daikon**	Japanese radish
かぶ kabboo **kabu**	turnip
しめじ shee-mej-ee **shimeji**	brown button mushrooms
えのき enno-kee **enoki**	pale yellow button mushrooms served in a bunch
白菜 hak-sye **hakusai**	Chinese cabbage
わさび wass-abbee **wasabi**	Japanese horseradish

[*For other essential expressions, see 'Shop talk', p. 69*]

Meat

ESSENTIAL INFORMATION

● Key words to look for:
  肉 (meat)
  肉店 (butcher)
● Weight guide: 4–6 oz/125–200 g of meat per person for one meal.
● Although butchers will provide cuts if requested, usually meats are pre-cut and packed.
● Pork, sausages, ham, liver, chicken and canned goods are plentiful and inexpensive.
● Lamb, mutton and turkey are very hard to find (though sometimes available at foreign food specialist shops).
● Beef is excellent but very expensive.
● Some restaurants feature duck, whalemeat, wild boar, rabbit and other 'exotic' dishes but these are not usually found in markets.

WHAT TO SAY

Some beef, please	牛肉ください ghee-oo nee-koo koo-dass-eye gyūniku kudasai
Some lamb	ラム lam-oo ramu
Some mutton	マトン mat-on maton
Some pork	豚肉 boo-ta nee-koo buta niku
Some veal	子牛肉 kaw-oosh-ee nee-koo koushi niku
Some steak	ステーキ肉 stair-kee nee-koo sutēkiniku
Some liver	肝臓 kan-zaw kanzō
Some kidneys	腎臓 jeen-zaw jinzō
Some sausages	ソーセージ saw-sair-jee sōsēji
Some minced meat	ひき肉 hee-kee-nee-koo hiki niku
Some pork chops	豚の骨付きあばら肉 boo-ta-no hon-ay-ts-kee ab-arra nee-koo buta no honetsuki abara niku
Some lamb chops	子羊の骨付きあばら肉 ko-heet-soo-jee no hon-ay-ts-kee- ab-arra nee-koo kohitsuji no honetsuki abara niku

You may also want:

A chicken	鶏肉 kay-nee-koo keiniku
A tongue	タン tan tan

Other essential expressions [*see also p. 69*]:

Please can you mince it?	ミンチにしてください meen-chee nee shtay koo-dass-eye minchi ni shite kudasai
Please can you dice it?	角切りにしてください kak-oo ghee-ree nee-shtay 　koo-dass-eye kakugiri ni shite kudasai
Please can you trim the fat?	脂をとってください ab-oorra o tot-tay koo-dass-eye abura o totte kudasai

Fish

ESSENTIAL INFORMATION

● The place to look for: 鮮魚店 (fish store) or
　鮮魚コーナー (fish section) in supermarkets and department stores.
● You can buy take-away sushi (sliced, raw fish on small slabs of
　marinated sticky rice) at sushi shops.
● Weight guide: 8 oz/250 g minimum per person, for one meal of
　fish bought on the bone.
　i.e. ½ kilo/500 g　for two people
　1 kilo　　　　　for four people
　1½ kilos　　　　for six people
● There is a very wide variety of fresh fish, shellfish, dried and
　canned fish available and items which are not normally part of the
　American diet are common to the Japanese, like eel and octopus.

WHAT TO SAY

½ kilo of...	……を500グラム
	...o gaw h-yak-oo goo-ram-oo
	...o gohyaku guramu
1 kilo of...	……を1キロ
	...o ee-chee kee-law
	...o ichi kiro
1½ kilos of...	……を2キロ
	...o ee-chee kee-law gaw h-yak-oo
	...o ni kiro gohyaku guramu
cod/haddock	たら
	tarra
	tara
turbot	かれい
	karray
	karei
carp	こい
	koy
	koi
octopus	たこ
	takko
	tako
halibut	ひらめ
	hee-ram-ay
	hirame
tuna	まくろ
	mag-oo-raw
	maguro
sardines	いわし
	ee-wa-shee
	iwashi
squid	いか
	ee-ka
	ika
pike	かます
	kam-ass-oo
	kamasu
salmon/trout eggs	イクラ
	ee-koorra
	ikura
shrimps	小えび
	kaw-ebbee
	koebi

oysters	かき kak-ee kaki
prawns	車えび koo-roo-ma-ebbee kuruma ebi
mussels	むらさきし moo-rass-ak-eeg-eye murasakigai

Large fish are usually sold by the slice:

One slice of...	……を 一切れ ...o shtoh kee-ray ...o hito kire
Two slices of...	……を 二切れ ...o f-tak-ee-ray ...o futa kire
Seven slices of...	……を七切れ ...nanna-kee-ray ...o nana kire
cod	たら tarra tara
eel	あなご/うなぎ an-aggo/oo-nag-ee anago/unagi
halibut	ひらめ hee-ram-ay hirame
Two slices of salmon	さけを 二切れ sak-ay o f-tak-ee-ray sake o futa kire

For some shellfish and 'frying pan' fish, specify the number you want:

A crab, please	かにを 一匹ください kanny o eep-pikky koo-dass-eye kani o ippiki kudasai
A lobster	伊勢えび ee-say-ebbee ise ebi
A plaice/flounder	かれい karray karei

A trout	ます mass-oo masu
A sole	舌びらめ shtab-ee-ram-ay shitabirame
A mackerel	さば sabba saba
A herring	にしん nee-sheen nishin

Other essential expressions [*see also p. 69*]

Please can you take the heads off?	頭をとってください att-amma o tot-tay koo-dass-eye atama o totte kudasai
Please can you clean them?	洗ってください arrat-tay koo-dass-eye aratte kudasai
Please can you fillet them?	切り身にしてください kee-ree-mee-nee shtay koo-dass-eye kirimi ni shite kudasai

Types of fish served in sushi shops:

A kind of mackerel	はまち ham-atch-ee hamachi
Tuna fish (red)	まぐろ mag-oo-raw maguro
Tuna fish (light pink)	ちゅうとろ choo-torraw chūtoro
A sardine-like fish (marinated)	こはだ ko-hadda kohada
Shrimp, prawn	えび eb-ee ebi

Conger eel (cooked)	あなご
	anna-go
	anago
Octopus	たこ
	takko
	tako
Squid	いか
	ee-ka
	ika
A horse mackerel	あじ
	ajjee
	aji
Orange eggs of the sea chestnut	うに
	oo-nee
	uni
Salmon or trout eggs	いくら
	ee-koorra
	ikura

[*For other essential expressions, see 'Shop talk', p. 69*]

Eating and drinking out
Ordering a drink

ESSENTIAL INFORMATION

- The places to look for: [*see p. 22*]
  喫茶/珈琲　(coffee shop)
  スナック　(a type of pub)
  バー　(bar)
- Be careful about bars outside your hotel (especially hostess bars) unless they have been recommended or you are with someone who knows the place. Otherwise it is easy to run up a very high bill in a short period of time.
- The bill comes when you are ready to leave, not after each drink.
- Tipping is not practiced and prices should be displayed somewhere (menu, window, wall).
- Service charges are included.
- During the summer months many department stores open beer gardens on the roof. Prices here are reasonable.
- Japanese brewed beer is similar in taste to German lager.
- Sake, the traditional Japanese drink, is brewed from rice that has been cooked with water and fermented. It is served hot in small pottery flasks which come in all shapes and sizes. There are several different grades and types of sake.

WHAT TO SAY

I'll have...please	……お願いします ...o-neg-eye-shee-mass ...onegai shimasu
a black coffee	ブラックコーヒー boo-rak kaw-hee burakku kōhī
a coffee with cream	クリーム入りコーヒー koo-reem eeree kaw-hee kurīmu iri kōhī
a tea with milk	ミルクティー meeroo-koo-tee miruku tī

a tea with lemon	レモンティー lem-on-tee remon tī
a glass of milk	ミルク mee-roo-koo miruku
two glasses of milk	ミルクをふたつ mee-roo-koo o f-tat-soo miruku o futatsu
a hot chocolate	ホットチョコレート hot-toh-chokko-rair-toh hotto chokorēto
a mineral water	ミネラルウォーター mee-nerral-wartah mineraru uōtā
a lemonade	レモネード lem-on-air-doh remonēdo
a Coca-Cola	コカコーラ kok-ka-kaw-la koka kōra
an orangeade	オレンジエード o-ren-jee air-doh orenjiēdo
a fresh orange juice	フレッシュ・オレンジジュース foo-lesh o-renj jooss furesshu orenji jūsu
a grape juice	グレープジュース goo-rair-poo jooss gurēpu jūsu
an apple juice	アップルジュース ap-poo-roo jooss appuru jūsu
a beer	ビール bee-roo bīru
a draught beer	生ビール namma-bee-roo nama bīru
a black beer	黒ビール koo-raw bee-roo kuro bīru

A glass of...	……をひとつ	
	...o shtots	
	...o hitotsu	
Two glasses of...	……をふたつ	
	...o f-tats	
	...o futatsu	
red wine	ホワイン	
	akka wye-een	
	aka wain	
white wine	白ワイン	
	shee-raw wye-een	
	shiro wain	
rosé wine	ロゼワイン	
	raw-zay-wye-een	
	roze wain	
dry	辛口	
	karra koo-chee	
	karakuchi	
sweet	甘口	
	amma koo-chee	
	amakuchi	
A bottle of...	……を一びん	
	...o shto-been	
	...o hitobin	
sparkling wine	スパークリング・ワイン	
	sparkoo-leeng wye-een	
	supākuringu wain	
champagne	シャンパン	
	sham-pan	
	shanpen	
A whisky with ice	オンザロック	
	on-zarrok	
	onzarokku	
A whisky with water	水割り	
	mee-zoo-arry	
	mizuwari	
A whisky with soda	ハイボール	
	high baw-roo	
	haibōru	
A gin with tonic	ジントニック	
	jeen-ton-eek	
	jintonikku	

A gin with bitter lemon	ジンレモン jeen-lem-on jinremon
A brandy/cognac	ブランデー/コニャック boo-ran-dair/kon-yak burandē/konyakku
A martini	マティーニ mattee-nee matīni
A sherry	シェリー shel-ee sherī

These are all types of sake which you may like to try:

日本酒（あつかん） nee-hon-shoo (ats-kan) nihonshu (atsukan)	rice wine (warm/hot)
日本酒（ひや） nee-hon-shoo (hee-ya) nihonshu (hiya)	rice wine (cold)
升酒 masser-zakkay masuzake	rice wine served in a small wooden box
地酒 jiz-akkay jizake	rice wine brewed by local country breweries
泡盛 awa-morry awamori	Okinawan strong distilled spirits
焼酎 shaw-choo shōchū	distilled spirit made from rice
麦焼酎 moo-ghee-shaw-choo mugishōchū	distilled spirit made from barley

Other essential expressions:

Miss!/Waiter!	すみません！ soo-mee mass-en sumimasen

The bill, please	お勘定お願いします
	o-kan-jaw on-eg-eye-shee-mass
	okanjō onegai shimasu
How much does that come to?	いくらになりますか
	ee-koorra nee narry-mass ka
	ikura ni narimasu ka
Is service included?	サービス料ははいっていますか
	sa-beess ree-aw wa height-tem-ass ka
	sābisuryō wa haitte imasu ka
Where is the toilet, please?	トイレはどこですか
	toy-ray wa dokko dess ka
	toire wa doko desu ka

Ordering a snack

ESSENTIAL INFORMATION

- In addition to a multitude of Japanese snack shops (noodle stands, etc.), there are also many Western-style food places such as hamburger, pizza and fried chicken shops.
- Coffee shops also serve food (sandwiches and cakes).
- Snack bars, スナック on the other hand, are primarily bars which also serve food and they usually stay open until quite late.
- Wherever you eat it is safe as high hygiene standards are maintained.
- For cakes, see p. 76.
- For ice cream, see p. 78.
- For picnic-type snacks, Japanese style, see p. 84.

WHAT TO SAY

I'll have...please	……お願いします ...o-neg-eye-shee-mass ...onegai shimasu
a cheese sandwich/roll	チーズサンドイッチ ロール cheez-sando-wee-chee/raw-loo chīzu sandoitchi/rōru
a ham sandwich/roll	ハムサンドイッチ ロール ham-oo sando-wee-chee/raw-loo hamu sandoitchi/rōru
a tuna sandwich/roll	ツナサンドイッチ ロール tsoonna sando-wee-chee/raw-loo tsuna sandoitchi/rōru
an omelet with mushrooms	マッシュルームオムレツ mash-roomoo omoo-lets masshurūmu omuretsu
an omelet with diced ham	ハムオムレツ ham-oo omoo-lets hamu omuretsu

There are some other snacks you may like to try:

ハンバーガー ham-bah-gah hambāgā	a Hamburger

スパゲティナポリタン
spag-ett-ee nap-ol-ee-tan
supagetī naporitan

a spaghetti seasoned with tomato
   sauce or ketchup

オムライス
om-ryess
omuraisu

seasoned rice with ketchup
   wrapped in thin fried egg

おにぎり
on-ee-ghirry
onigiri

rice ball wrapped in seaweed
   with fish roe or a salted plum
   in the centre

そば
sobba
soba

buckwheat noodles in soup

ラーメン
lah-men
rāmen

Chinese noodles in soup

You may want to add to your order:

with..., please

……をつけてください
...o t-sket-ay koo-dass-eye
...o tsukete kudasai

   bread

ハン
pan
pan

   french fries

フライド・ホテト
foo-rye-doh pot-etto
furaido poteto

   potato salad

ホテトサラダ
pot-etto sal-adda
poteto sarada

   mustard

マスタード
mass-tahdo
masutādo

   ketchup

ケチャッソ
ketch-ap-oo
kechappu

   mayonnaise

マヨネーズ
ma-yonnair-zoo
mayonēzu

[*For other essential expressions, see 'Ordering a drink' p. 98*]

In a restaurant

ESSENTIAL INFORMATION

● The place to look for: レストラン [*see p. 22*]
● You can eat at these places:

レストラン　(restaurant)
グリル　(grill)
軽食堂　(family eating place Japanese and Western food available)
喫茶店　(coffee shop)
スナック　(local bar which also serves snacks)
寿司屋　(sushi)
小料理　(Japanese restaurant)
割烹　(Japanese restaurant—more expensive than one above)

● Many restaurants will give the 'menu' (with prices) in the front window in the form of plastic replicas of the dishes so you can really see what you'll be getting (and they're quite realistic!). If there is a language problem, all you have to do is point.
● Self-service is rare but can be the rule in the cafeterias of the so-called business hotels.
● Some offer special dishes for young children: お子様ランチ (okkoss-amma lan-chee/okosama ranchi)
● The top or upper floors of the big department stores are often given over to restaurants of all kinds.
● Beer gardens on roofs of department stores are favourite cooling-off places in the hot summer months.
● In Japanese cuisine restaurants beer and sake are widely served.
● Tea comes free after the meal in many Japanese-style restaurants and you can have as much as you want.
● In many Japanese-style restaurants there are counters where the food is laid out in front of you and you gesture to the cook which particular dish you want.
● Most restautants have set lunches. Ask for ランチ (lan-chee/ranchi).
● Most restaurants offer hot or cold towels (depending on the season) to wipe your hands and face with before the meal.
● You can also find almost any other international cuisine in the metropolitan areas.
● Wherever you go, tipping is unnecessary. Service charges are usually included.

How to use chopsticks

Place first chopstick
between base of
thumb and top of ring
finger.

Hold second chop-
stick between top of
the thumb and tops
of middle and index
fingers.

Keeping the first
chopstick and thumb
still, move the other
one up and down by
middle and index
fingers.

WHAT TO SAY

May I book a table?
席を予約できますか
sek-ee o yoy-akkoo dek-ee-mass ka
seki o yoyaku dekimasu ka

I've booked a table
予約してあります
yoy-akkoo shtay arry-mass
yoyaku shite arimasu

A table for one
一人用のテーブル
sh-torry-yaw no tay-boo-roo
hitoriyō no tēburu

A table for three
三人用のテーブル
san-neen yaw no tay-boo-roo
sanninyō no tēburu

The à la carte menu, please
アラカルトメニューお願いします
alla-karroo-toh men-yoo o-neg-eye-shee-mass
arakaruto menyū onegai shimasu

The fixed-price menu
定食のメニュー
tay-shok-oo no men-yoo
teishoku no menyu

Today's special menu	きょうの特別メニュー
	kee-aw no tok-oo bets men-yoo
	kyō no tokubetsu menyū
What's this, please [*point to menu*]	これはなんですか
	korray wa nan dess ka
	kore wa nan desu ka
The wine list	ワインリスト
	wye-een leesto
	wain risuto
A carafe of wine, please	デカンタのワインをください
	dek-anta no wye-een o koo-dass-eye
	dekanta no wain o kudasai
A glass of wine, please	ワインを一杯ください
	wye-een o eep-pye koo-dass-eye
	wain o ippai kudasai
A bottle	一びん
	shto-been
	hitobin
A half bottle	ハーフボトル
	ha-f-bot-orroo
	hāfubotoru
A litre	1リットル
	ee-chee leet-olloo
	ichi rittoru
Red/white/rosé/house wine	赤/白/ロゼ/ハウスワイン
	akka/shee-raw/raw-zay/howss-wye-een
	aka/shiro/roze/hausu wain
Some more bread, please	もうすこしパンをください
	maw skosh-ee pan o koo-dass-eye
	mō sukoshi pan o kudasai
Some more wine, please	もうすこしワインをください
	maw skosh-ee wye-een o koo-dass-eye
	mō sukoshi wain o kudasai
Some oil	油
	ab-oorra
	abura
Some salt	塩
	shee-aw
	shio

Some pepper	コショウ koshaw koshō
Some vinegar	酢 soo su
Some water	水 mee-zoo mizu
How much does that come to?	いくらになりますか ee-koorra nee narry-mass ka ikura ni narimasu ka
Is service included?	サービス料ははいっていますか sa-beess ree-aw wa height-tem-ass ka sābisuryō wa haitte imasu ka
Where is the toilet, please?	お手洗はどこですか o-tay-ar-rye wa dokko dess ka otearai wa doko desu ka
Miss!/Waiter!	すみません！ soo-mee-mass-en sumimasen
The bill, please	お勘定お願いします o-kan-jaw o-neg-eye-shee-kass okanjō onegai shimasu

Key words for courses, as seen on some menus. [*Only ask this question if you want the waiter to remind you of the choice.*]

What have you got in the way of...	……になにがありますか ...nee nannee ga arry-mass ka ...ni nani ga arimasu ka
STARTERS/ HORS D'OEUVRES?	スターター オードブル stah-tah/awd-er-boo-roo sutātā/odoburu
SOUP?	スープ soo-poo sūpu
EGG DISHES?	卵料理 tam-aggo ree-aw-ree tamago ryōri
FISH?	魚料理 sak-anna ree-aw-ree sakana ryōri

MEAT?	肉料理 nee-koo ree-aw-ree niku ryōri
GAME/POULTRY?	鳥料理 torry ree-aw-ree tori ryori
VEGETABLES?	野菜 yass-eye yasai
CHEESE?	チーズ chee-zoo chīzu
FRUIT?	フルーツ f-root-soo furūtsu
ICE CREAM?	アイスクリーム eye-ss-koo-ree-moo aisukurīmu
DESSERT?	デザート dez-ah-toh dezāto

UNDERSTANDING THE MENU

● You will find the names of the principal ingredients of most dishes
  on these pages:

Starters, see p. 84   Fruit, see p. 87
Meat, see p. 91   Dessert, see p. 78
Fish, see p. 93   Cheese, see p. 84
Vegetables, see p. 87   Ice cream, see p. 78

  Used together with the following lists of cooking and menu terms,
  they should help you to decode the menu.

● These cooking and menu terms are for understanding only — not
  for speaking aloud.

Cooking and menu terms

お好み焼き o-kon-om-ee-yak-ee okonomiyaki	pancake with vegetables, meat, fish etc. cooked on a griddle at the table
会席 懐石 **kye-sek-ee** **kaiseki**	traditional vegetarian and very expensive dishes served on lacquer trays

カツレツ
kats-oo-rets-oo
katsuretsu

cutlets (pork, chicken, beef)

串焼き
koo-shee-yak-ee
kushiyaki

skewers of meat, fish and vegetables grilled over charcoal

くん製
koon-say
kunsei

smoked

刺身
sash-ee-mee
sashimi

slices of raw fish of various kinds

塩焼き
shee-aw-yak-ee
shioyaki

small whole fish broiled in salt

しゃぶしゃぶ
shab-oo-shab-oo
shabushabu

vegetables and thin slices of beef boiled and eaten with various dips

すき焼き
skee-yak-ee
sukiyaki

vegetables and thin slices of beef cooked in a soy sauce, sugar and sake stock

すし
soo-shee
sushi

slices of raw fish on marinated rice mounds

茶碗むし
cha-wan-moo-shee
chawanmushi

a dish made with fish broth and eggs of the consistency of blancmange

鉄板焼き
tep-pan-yak-ee
teppanyaki

meat, fish and vegetables grilled at the table

照り焼き
terry-yak-ee
teriyaki

fish fillet broiled with soy sauce and sake

てんぷら
tem-poorra
tempura

light and deep-fried fish and vegetables

なべ
nab-ay
nabe

fish, meat and vegetables all boiled together in a large earthenware pot

幕の内
mak-oo-no-oo-chee
makunouchi

cold rice, vegetables, fish or meat served in a box

水たき
mee-zoo-tak-ee
mizutaki

chicken and vegetables boiled in a large earthen pot at the table

焼き鳥
yak-ee torry
yakitori

skewers of chicken/duck/quail dipped in sweet soy sauce and cooked over charcoal grill

炉ばた焼き
rob-atta-yak-ee
robatayaki

meat, fish and vegetables grilled over charcoal

Further words to help you understand the menu

うなぎ丼
oo-na-ghee-dom-boo-ree
unagi domburi

broiled eel on rice in a bowl

うな重
oonaj-oo
unajū

broiled eel on rice in a lacquered box

お茶漬
ochaz-oo-kay
ochazuke

a bowl of rice in a fish or tea broth

おひたし
oshee-tash-ee
ohitashi

boiled spinach or green vegetables with sesame seeds or dried flakes of bonito

きつねうどん
keet-soonay oodon
kitsune udon

wheat flour noodles in a fish broth with soy sauce seasoning and fried bean curd

きんぴらごぼう
kin-pirra-gob-aw
kinpiragobō

fried burdock root and carrot strips

ごはん
go-han
gohan

rice

ざるそば
zarroo-sobba
zarusoba

boiled cold buckwheat noodles on a bamboo rack in a lacquered box

酢の物
soo-no-monno
sunomono

vegetables with raw fish and seasoned with sugar and vinegar

ぞうすい
zaw-see
zōsui

rice boiled in a soy sauce seasoned soup

チキンカツ chik-keen-kats chikinkatsu	deep-fried breaded chicken cutlet
チャーハン chah-han chāhan	fried rice with small pieces of meat and vegetables
田楽 den-gak-oo dengaku	rectangles of soy bean curd on bamboo skewers covered with sauces and charcoal broiled
天丼 ten-don tendon	bowl of rice with tempura (see above under 'Cooking and menu terms') shrimps on top
天ぷらそば tem-poo-ra sobba tempura soba	a bowl of buckwheat noodles in a fish bouillon broth with deep-fried tempura shrimp
トンカツ ton-kats tonkatsu	deep fried breaded pork cutlet
納豆 nat-taw nattō	sticky fermented soy bean paste seasoned with soy sauce and leek
冷奴 hee-ya-yak-kaw hiyayakko	cubes of cold bean curd with leek and ginger
味噌汁 mee-sow-shirroo misoshiru	fish bouillon and fermented bean paste based soup
焼肉 yak-ee nee-koo yakiniku	thin slices of marinated fried pork
野菜煮つけ yass-sye neet-skay yasai nitsuke	cold dish of cooked seasonal vegetables

Health

ESSENTIAL INFORMATION

- Advice on doctors and services can be obtained through your embassy in Tokyo and clinics/hospitals catering for foreigners in particular can be found in the yellow pages directory in your hotel.
- It is *essential* to have proper medical insurance as medical care in Japan is very expensive.
- However, if you are planning on being in Japan for a considerable period of time, it would be advisable to join the National Health Insurance programme (Kokumin Kenko Hoken) in order to save on costs.
- Take your own first aid kit with you.
- It is wise to bring the medicines you are likely to need with you in case they are not readily available in the same form in Japan. It is also a good idea to carry a data card on your person in case of an emergency, especially one showing your blood type.
- For minor disorders and treatment at a drugstore, see p. 48.
- For finding your way to a doctor, dentist, or drugstore, see p. 22.
- Once in Japan decide on a definite plan of action in case of serious illness: communicate your problem to a near neighbour, the receptionist or someone you see regularly. You are then dependent on that person helping you obtain treatment.
- If you need a doctor look for:

| 医者 | (doctor) | 病院 | (hospital) |
| 外科 | (surgery) | 国民健康保険 | (national health insurance) |

What's the matter?

I have a pain in my... ……が痛いんです
...ga ee-tine-dess
... ga itai n desu

abdomen おなか
on-akka
onaka

ankle くるぶし
kurroo-boo-shee
kurubushi

I have a pain in my... ……が痛いんです
...ga ee-tine-dess
...ga itai n desu

arm	腕
	oo-day
	ude
back	背中
	sen-akka
	senaka
bladder	膀胱
	baw-kaw
	bōkō
bowels	腸
	chaw
	chō
breast	乳房
	chee-boo-sah
	chibusa
chest	胸
	moo-nay
	mune
ear	耳
	mee-mee
	mimi
eye	目
	may
	me
foot	足
	ash-ee
	ashi
head	頭
	at-amma
	atama
heel	踵
	kak-atto
	kakato
jaw	あご
	agg-aw
	ago
kidney	腎臓
	jeen-zaw
	jinzō

leg	脚
	ash-ee
	ashi
lung	肺
	high
	hai
neck	首
	koo-bee
	kubi
penis	ペニス
	pen-eess
	penisu
shoulder	肩
	kata
	kata
stomach	胃
	ee
	i
testicle	睾丸
	kaw-gan
	kōgan
throat	喉
	noddo
	nodo
vagina	膣
	cheet-soo
	chitsu
wrist	手首
	tek-oo-bee
	tekubi

I have a pain here [*point*]	ここが痛いんです
	kokko ga ee-tine dess
	koko ga itai n desu
I have a toothache	歯が痛いんです
	hagga ee-tine dess
	ha ga itai n desu
I have broken...	……がこわれました
	..ga ko-warray-mash-ta
	...ga kowaremashita
my dentures/glasses	入れ歯　めがね
	ee-rebba/meg-an-ay
	ireba/megane

I have lost...　　　　　　　　……をなくしました
　　　　　　　　　　　　　...o nak-shee-mash-ta
　　　　　　　　　　　　　...o nakushimashita

　　my contact lenses　　　コンタクトレンズ
　　　　　　　　　　　　　kon-tak-tollenz
　　　　　　　　　　　　　kontakuto renzu

　　a filling　　　　　　　詰め物
　　　　　　　　　　　　　tsoo-mem-onno
　　　　　　　　　　　　　tsumemono

My child is ill　　　　　子どもの具合が悪いんです
　　　　　　　　　　　　　kod-ommo no goo-eye ga wa-reen
　　　　　　　　　　　　　　dess
　　　　　　　　　　　　　kodomo no guai ga warui n
　　　　　　　　　　　　　　desu

He/she has a pain in　　彼/彼女は……が痛いんです
his/her...　　　　　　　karray/kanno-jaw wa...ga ee-tine
　　　　　　　　　　　　　　dess
　　　　　　　　　　　　　kare/kanojo wa...ga itai n
　　　　　　　　　　　　　　desu

　　ankle [see list above]　くるぶし
　　　　　　　　　　　　　kurroo-boo-shee
　　　　　　　　　　　　　kurubushi

How bad is it?

I'm ill　　　　　　　　　　具合が悪いんです
　　　　　　　　　　　　　goo-eye ga warreen dess
　　　　　　　　　　　　　guai ga warui n desu

It's urgent　　　　　　　　緊急です
　　　　　　　　　　　　　keen-kew dess
　　　　　　　　　　　　　kinkyū desu

It's serious　　　　　　　　ひどいんです
　　　　　　　　　　　　　hee-doyn dess
　　　　　　　　　　　　　hidoi n desu

It's not serious　　　　　　そんなにひどくないです
　　　　　　　　　　　　　son-na-nee hee-dok-oo nine dess
　　　　　　　　　　　　　sonna ni hidoku nai n desu

It hurts　　　　　　　　痛みます
　　　　　　　　　　　　　ee-tam-ee-mass
　　　　　　　　　　　　　itamimasu

It hurts a lot　　　　　　ひどく痛みます
　　　　　　　　　　　　　hee-dok-oo ee-tam-ee-mass
　　　　　　　　　　　　　hidoku itamimasu

It doesn't hurt much	あまり痛みません
	amma-ree ee-tam-ee-mass-en
	amari itamimasen
The pain occurs...	……痛みます
	...ee-tam-ee-mass
	...itamimasu
every quarter of an hour	15分おきに
	joo-gaw-foon aw-kee-nee
	jūgohun oki ni
every half-hour	30分おきに
	san jip-poon aw-kee-nee
	sanjippun oki ni
every hour	1時間おきに
	ee-chee-jee kan aw-kee-nee
	ichi jikan oki ni
every day	1日おきに
	ee-chee-nee-chee aw-kee nee
	ichi nichi oki ni
It hurts most of the time	だいたいずっと痛みます
	dye-tye zert-taw ee-tam-ee-mass
	daitai zutto itamimasu
I've had it for...	……つづいています
	...tsoo-zoo-ee-tay-ee-mass
	...tsuzuite imasu
one hour/one day	1時間/1日
	ee-chee-jee-kan/ee-chee-nee-chee
	ichi jikan/ichi nichi
two hours/two days	2時間/ふつか
	nee-jee-kan/f-tska
	ni jikan/futsuka
It's a...	……です
	...dess
	...desu
sharp pain	鋭い痛み
	soo-roo-doy ee-tam-ee
	surudoi itami
dull ache (pain)	鈍い痛み
	nee-boo-ee ee-tam-ee
	nibui itami
nagging pain	しじゅう痛い
	shee-joo ee-tie
	shijū itai

I/he/she feel(s)...	私は/彼は/彼女は……
	wattash-ee wa/karray wa/kanno-jaw wa...
	watashi wa/kare wa/kanojo wa ...
dizzy	目まいがします
	mem-eye ga shee-mass
	memai ga shimasu
sick	気分が悪いんです
	kee-boon ga warreen dess
	kibun ga warui n desu
weak	だるいんです
	darroo-een dess
	darui n desu
feverish	熱があります
	netsoo ga arry-mass
	netsu ga arimasu

Already under treatment for something else?

I take...regularly [*show*]	……をいつも飲んでいます
	...o eetsoo maw non-day-ee-mass
	...o itsumo nonde imasu
this medicine	この薬
	konno k-soo-ree
	kono kusuri
these pills	この錠剤
	konno jaw-zye
	kono jōzai
I have...	……の気があります
	...no kegga arry-mass
	...no ke ga arimasu
a heart condition	心臓病
	sheen-zawb-yaw
	shinzōbyō
haemorrhoids	痔
	jee
	ji
rheumatism	リューマチ
	ree-oo-match-ee
	ryūmachi

I am...	私は……です
	wattash-ee wa...dess
	watashi wa...desu
diabetic	糖尿病
	tawn-yawb-yaw
	tōnyōbyō
asthmatic	喘息
	zen-sok-oo
	zensoku
allergic to (penicillin)	(ペニシリン)に対してアレルギーです
	(pen-ee-shee-reen) nee tye-shtay al-air-oo-ghee dess
	(penishirin) ni taishite arerugī desu
I am pregnant	私は妊娠しています
	wattash-ee-wa neen-sheen-shtay-ee-mass
	watashi wa ninshin shite imasu

Other essential expressions

Please can you help?	お願いできますか
	on-eg-eye-dek-ee-mass ka
	onegai dekimasu ka
A doctor, please	医者をお願いします
	ee-sha o on-eg-eye-shee-mass
	isha o onegai shimasu
A dentist	歯医者
	high-sha
	haisha
I don't speak Japanese	日本語が話せません
	nee-hon-go ga han-assem-ass-en
	nihongo ga hanasemasen
What time does...arrive?	……は何時に来られますか
	...wa nan-jee nee korrar-em-ass ka
	...wa nanji ni koraremasu ka
the doctor/the dentist	医者 歯医者
	ee-sha/high-sha
	isha/haisha

From the doctor: key sentences to understand

Take this...	これを……飲んでください
	korray o ...non-day koo-dass-eye
	kore o...nonde kudasai
every day	毎日
	my-nee-chee
	mainichi
every hour	1時間おきに
	ee-chee-jee kan aw-kee nee
	ichi jikan oki ni
four times a day	1日4回
	ee-chee-nee-chee yon-kye
	ichi nichi yonkai
Stay in bed	床から出ないでください
	tokko karra den-eye-dek-oo dass-eye
	toko kara denaide kudasai
Don't travel...	旅行をしないでください
	ree-aw-kaw o shee-nye-dek-oo-dass-eye
	ryokō o shinaide kudasai
for...days/weeks	……日間/週間
	...nee-chee-kan/shoo-kan
	...nichikan/shūkan
You must go to hospital	入院しなければいけません
	new-een shee-na-kerrebba ee-kem-ass-en
	nyūin shinakereba ikemasen

Problems: complaints, loss, theft

ESSENTIAL INFORMATION

● Problems with:
camping facilities, see p. 46.
household appliances, see p. 66
health, see p. 113
the car, see p. 132
● If the worst comes to the worst, find a police box (a policeman will always be on duty) or police station. To ask the way, see p. 22.
● Look for:
警察署 (police station)
交番 (police box) each box has a red light on it.
● If you lose your passport report the loss to the police and go to the American Embassy.
● In an emergency, dial 110 for police and 119 for fire and ambulance. Railway stations have lost and found offices.
● The average Japanese is honest and Japan is probably among the safer countries in the world.
● If something is left behind in a taxi or on a train, it will probably be handed in to a nearby police box or station.

COMPLAINTS

I bought this...	これを……買いました
	korray-o kye-mash-ta
	kore o...kaimashita
today	きょう
	kee-aw
	kyō
yesterday	きのう
	kee-naw
	kinō
on Monday (see p. 161)	月曜日に
	ghets-yaw-bee nee
	getsuyōbi ni
last week	先週
	senshoo
	senshū

It's no good (unsuitable)	ちょっと気に入らないんです
	chot-taw kee-nee ee-ran-ine dess
	chotto ki ni iranai n desu
It's no good (faulty)	ちょっとおかしいんです
	chot-taw ok-ash-een dess
	chotto okashii n desu
Look	見てください
	mee-tay koo-dass-eye
	mite kudasai
Here [*point*]	ここです
	kokko dess
	koko desu
Can you...	……いただけますか
	...ee-taddak-em-ass ka
	...itadakemasu ka
change it?	かえて
	kye-ettay
	kaete
mend it?	修理して
	shoo-ree-shtay
	shūri shite
give me a refund?	お金を返して
	o-kan-ay o kye-eshtay
	okane o kaeshite
Here's the receipt	これがレシートです
	korray ga resheeto dess
	kore ga reshīto desu
Can I see the manager?	店長と話したいのですが
	tenchaw toh hanash-tye-no-dess ga
	tenchō to hanashitai no desu ga

LOSS
[*See also 'Theft' below: the lists are interchangeable*]

I have lost...	……をなくしました
	...o nak-shee-mash-ta
	...o nakushimashita
my bag	カバン
	kab-an
	kaban
my bracelet	ブレスレット
	bress-ret-ta
	buresuretto

my camera	カメラ kamerra kamera	
my car keys	車のカギ koo-roo-ma no kaggy kuruma no kagi	
my car logbook	自動車旅行日誌 jeedaw-sha ree-awkaw neesh-shee jidōsha ryokō nisshi	
my driver's license	運転免許証 oonten menk-yaw-shaw unten menkyoshō	
my insurance certificate	保険証書 hokken shaw-shaw hoken shōsho	
my jewelry	宝石 haw-sek-ee hōseki	
everything	持ち物ぜんぶ motch-ee monno zen-boo mochimono zenbu	

THEFT
[*See also 'Loss' above: the lists are interchangeable*]

Someone has stolen...	……を盗まれました ...o noo-soo-marray-mash-ta ...o nusumaremashita	
my car	車 koo-roo-ma kuruma	
my car radio	カーラジオ kah-raj-ee-o kārajio	
my luggage	荷物 nee-mots nimotsu	
my money	お金 o-kan-ay okane	
my necklace	ネックレス nek-koo-ress nekkuresu	

Someone has stolen...	……を盗まれました
	...o noo-soo-marray-mash-ta
	...o nusumaremashita
my passport	パスポート
	passpawto
	pasupōto
my radio	ラジオ
	raj-ee-o
	rajio
my tickets	切符
	keep-poo
	kippu
my traveler's checks	トラベラーズチェック
	tol-ab-ellarz chek-koo
	toraberāzu chekku
my wallet/watch	さいふ／時計
	sye-foo/tok-air
	saifu/tokei

LIKELY REACTIONS

Wait	ちょっと待ってください
	chot-taw mat-tay koo-dass-eye
	chotto matte kudasai
When?	いつですか
	eets dess-ka
	itsu desu ka
Where?	どこですか
	dokko dess-ka
	doko desu ka
Name?	お名前は
	onna-my wa
	onamae wa
Address?	住所は
	joo-shaw wa
	jūsho wa
I can't help you	申し訳ありませんが
	maw-shee-wakkay arry-mass-en ga
	mōshiwake arimasen ga
Nothing to do with me	私のほうでは責任を負いかねます
	wattash-ee no haw day wa sek-ee-neen o oy-kan-ay-mass
	watashi no hō de wa sekinin o oikanemasu

The post office

ESSENTIAL INFORMATION

- To find a post office, see p. 22.
- Key words to look for:
  郵便局 (post office)
  身分証明書 (ID card)
  留置き (poste restante)
- Look for this sign:

Post Office Sign

- Stamps are sold in places other than post offices and you will know them by the fact that an orange letter box with the above sign will be in front or nearby.
- Blue letter boxes are for express mail.
- Poste restante (general delivery) arrangements are the same in any post office in Japan. Letters are held for one month only. When collecting mail, the recipient must show some identification, such as passport, driver's licence (you will be asked for your ID card mee-boon shaw-may-shaw/mibunshomeisho).
- The Japanese words for poste restante are given above (pronounced tommay aw-kee/tome oki); it would help if the sender could write them on the envelope. And it would probably be advisable to ask anyone writing to you to ensure that they print the address clearly on the envelope.
- Post offices are open from 9 a.m. to 5 p.m. except Saturday afternoons and Sundays.

WHAT TO SAY

To England, please [*Hand letters, cards or parcels over the counter*]	イギリスお願いします ee-ghee-reesser on-eg-eye-shee-mass igirisu onegai shimasu
To Australia	オーストラリア awss-taw-rall-ya ōsutoraria
To New Zealand	ニュージーランド new jee-lando nyūjīrando
To the United States	アメリカ am-ellee-ka amerika

To Canada	カナダ
[*For other countries,*	kan-adda
see p. 168]	kanada
How much is...	……はいくらですか
	...wa ee-koorra dess-ka
	...wa ikura desu ka
this parcel (to Canada)?	このカナダへの小包み
	konno kan-adda-ay no koz-oo-tsoo-mee
	kono kanada e no kozutsumi
a letter (to Australia)?	オーストラリアへの手紙
	awss-taw-rall-ya-ay-no teg-am-ee
	ōsutoraria e no tegami
a postcard (to England)?	英国へのハガキ
	ay-kok-oo-ay no hag-akky
	eikoku e no hagaki
Air mail	航空便
	kaw-koo-been
	kōkūbin
Surface mail	普通便/船便
	f-tsoo-been/foona-been
	futsūbin/funabin
Express mail	速達
	sok-tats
	sokutatsu
One stamp, please	切手を一枚ください
	keet-tay o eechee-my koo-dass-eye
	kitte o ichimai
Two stamps	切手を二枚
	keet-tay o nee-my
	kitte o nimai
One (300 yen) stamp, please	300円切手を一枚ください
	sanb-yak-oo-en keet-tay o eechee-my koo-dass-eye
	sambyakuen kitte o ichimai kudasai
I'd like to send a telegram	電報を打ちたいのですが
	den-paw o ooch-tie no dess ga
	denpō o uchitai no desu

Where's the poste restante?	局留め郵便の窓口はどこですか
	kee-ok-oo-dom-ay yoo-been no maddo-goo-chee wa dokko dess ka
	kyokudomeyūbin no madoguchi wa doko desu ka
Is there any mail for me?	私宛てに郵便がきていますか
	wattash-ee atten-ee yoo-been ga kee-tay-ee-mass ka
	watashiate ni yūbin ga kite imasu ka

Telephoning

ESSENTIAL INFORMATION

- The 10 yen coin is used for 3 minute calls *within* any area.
- You can use any of the various coloured public phones (red, blue, green, yellow or pink) for this purpose.
- This is how to use a public telephone:
  —take off the receiver
  —insert the money
  —dial the number (unused coins will be refunded)
  —when your time is up, you will hear a warning buzzer; just insert more coins.
- For calls *outside* a particular area, insert as many 10 yen coins as you can (5 or 6) or use the yellow phone which takes 100 yen coins.
- A pink phone is not really a public phone but a private one found in coffee shops, doctors' offices, etc. However, anyone can use it by putting money in.
- For emergency calls 119 is the number for ambulance or fire and 110 for police. Yellow and blue phones can be used for emergency phone calls without charge.
- For international calls, it is best to use a private phone. Dial 0051 and the English-speaking operator will help you.

WHAT TO SAY

Where can I make a tele-phone call?	電話をかけたいのですが〝 den-wa o kak-et-eye-no dess ga denwa o kaketai no desu ga
Local/abroad	国内/海外 kok-oo-nye/kye-gye kokunai/kaigai
I'd like this number... [*show number*]	……この番号にかけたいんです ...konno ban-gaw nee kak-et-eye-n-dess ...kono bangō ni kaketai n desu
in England	英国の ay-kok-oo no eikoku no
in Canada	カナダの kan-adda no kanada no
in the USA [*For other countries, see p. 168*]	アメリカの am-ellee-ka no amerika no
Can you dial it for me, please?	かけていただけますか kak-et-ay-ee-taddak-em-ass ka kakete itadakemasu ka
How much is it?	いくらですか ee-koorra dess-ka ikura desu ka
Hello!	もしもし mosh-ee mosh-ee moshimoshi
May I speak to...?	……とお話したいのですが ...toh o-hanash-tie-no dess ga ...to ohanashi shitai no desu ga
Extension..., please	内線……お願いします nye-sen...o-neg-eye shee-mass naisen...onegai shimasu
I'm sorry, I don't speak Japanese	すみません日本語がわかりません soo-mee-mass-en nee-hon-go ga wak-arry-mass-en sumimasen nihongo ga wakarimasen
Do you speak English?	英語が話せますか ay-go ga hanass-em-ass-ka eigo ga hanasemasu ka

Thank you, I'll phone back	ありがとう、あとでまたかけます
	arry-gattaw atto day matta kak-em-ass
	arigatō ato de mata kakemasu
Good-bye	ごめんください
	gom-en koo-dass-eye
	gomen kudasai

LIKELY REACTIONS

That's (2000) yen	（二千）円です
	nee-sen-en dess
	(nisen) en desu
Cabin number (3)	（3 番）です
	san-ban-dess
	(san) ban desu
[*For numbers, see p. 154*]	
Please hang up and wait	いちど切ってお待ちください
	ee-chee daw keet-tay o-match-ee koo-dass-eye
	ichido kitte omachi kudasai
I'm trying to connect you	おつなぎします
	o-tsoo-nag-ee-shee-mass
	otsunagi shimasu
The line is engaged	お話し中です
	o-han-ash-chew dess
	ohanashichū desu
There's no answer	お返事がありません
	o-hen-jee ga arry-mass-en
	ohenji ga arimasen
You're through	どうぞお話しください
	daw-zaw o-hanash-ee koo-dass-eye
	dōzo ohanashi kudasai
There's a delay	ちょっと通じないのでお待ちください
	chot-taw tsoo-jee-nye-no day o-match-ee koo-dass-eye
	chotto tsūjinai node omachi kudasai
There's a telephone call for you	（……さん）お電話です
	(...san) oden-wa dess
	(...san) odenwa desu

Cashing checks and changing money

ESSENTIAL INFORMATION

- Finding your way to a bank or change bureau, see p. 22.
- Look for these words on buildings:
  銀行　　(bank)
  外国為替 (foreign exchange)
- To cash personal checks takes many weeks so it is best to carry traveler's checks, which can be exchanged at most main offices and branch offices of major banks in metropolitan areas. Fewer provincial banks provide this service, so make sure you don't run out of cash when out of town.
- Be prepared for up to a 15 minute wait when cashing checks.
- Have your passport handy.
- Banks are open from 9 a.m. to 3 p.m. on weekdays, 9 a.m. to 12 noon on Saturdays.
- You can also cash traveler's checks at a hotel but some require you to be resident there and the rate at hotels is not as good as at the banks.
- Wherever you are, the rate for traveler's checks is better than that for that for cash.
- To ask if a bank has a foreign exchange department,
  外為ありますか (gye-tam-ay arry-mass ka/gaitame arimasu ka),
  ask the floor manager (they usually wear armbands).

WHAT TO SAY

I'd like to cash...	……を現金にかえてください
	...o ghen-keen nee kye-et-ay koo-dass-eye
	...o genkin ni kaete kudasai
this/these traveler's check(s)	このトラベラーズチェック
	konno tol-ab-ellarz chek-koo
	kono toraberāzu chekku
this check	この小切手
	konno kog-eet-tay
	kono kogitte

I'd like to change this into Japanese yen

これを円にかえてください

korray o en nee kye-et-ay koo-dass-eye

kore o en ni kaete kudasai

Here's my passport

これが私のパスポートです

korray ga wattash-ee no passpawto dess

kore ga watashi no pasupōto desu

For travel into other countries

I'd like to change this... [*show bank notes*]

これを……にかえてください

korray o...nee kye-et-ay koo-dass-eye

kore o...ni kaete kudasai

into Hong Kong dollars

ホンコンのドル

hon-kon no dorroo

honkon no doru

into American dollars

アメリカのドル

am-ellee-ka no dorroo

amerika no doru

into Australian dollars

オーストラリアのドル

awss-taw-rall-ya no dorroo

ōsutoraria no doru

What's the rate of exchange?

交換レートはいくらですか

kaw-kan rair-toh wa ee-koorra dess ka

kōkan rēto wa ikura desu ka

LIKELY REACTIONS

Passport, please

パスポートを見せてください

passpawto o mee-set-ay koo-dass-eye

pasupōto o misete kudasai

Sign here

ここにサインしてください

kokko nee sign shtay koo-dass-eye

koko ni sain shite kudasai

Car travel

ESSENTIAL INFORMATION

- Finding a filling station or garage, see p. 22.
- There are no self-service stations in Japan.
- Grades of gasoline: for all practical purposes the only kind of gas used is standard (regular).
- 1 gallon is about 4½ litres (accurate enough up to 6 gallons).
- Filling stations can handle minor mechanical problems; for major repairs you have to find a garage. Look for ガレージ or 修理 (所)
- You must have an international driving license.
- There are plenty of rent-a-car agencies (レンタカー) and comprehensive insurance (including driver and passengers) is always included.
- Driving under the influence of alcohol is absolutely prohibited.
- Parking in large cities is troublesome and expensive.
- The Japan Automobile Federation (**JAF**) offers assistance to foreign motorists free of charge in case of a breakdown or an emergency.
- Japan drives on the left; road signs are international but expressway and other signs giving names of places, exits, etc. are mostly in Japanese.
- Unfamiliar road signs and warnings, see p. 152.

WHAT TO SAY
[*For numbers, see p. 154*]

(9) litres of...	……を9リットル
	...o kee-oo leet-olloo
	...o kyū rittoru
(2000) yen of...	……を二千円分
	...o nee seng yen boon
	...o nisen'en bun
standard/regular	無鉛
	moo-en
	muen
premium	ハイオクタン
	high-ok-tan
	haiokutan

diesel	軽油 kay-yoo keiyu
Fill it up, please	満タンにしてください man-tang nee shtay koo-dass-eye mantan ni shite kudasai
Will you check...	……を点検してください ...o teng-ken shtay koo-dass-eye ...o tenken shite kudasai
the oil?	オイル oy-loo oiru
the battery?	バッテリー bat-tel-ee batterī
the radiator?	ラジエーター laj-ee-air-tah rajiētā
the tires?	タイヤ tie-ya taiya
I've run out of gasoline	ガソリンがなくなりました gas-aw-leen ga nak-oo-narry-mash ta gasorin ga nakunarimashita
Can I borrow a can, please?	カンをお借りできますか kan o o-karry dek-ee-mass-ka kan o okari dekimasu ka
My car has broken down	車が故障しました koo-roo-ma ga kosh-aw shee-mash-ta kuruma ga koshō shimashita
My car won't start	エンジンがかかりません en-jeen ga kakka-ree-mass-en enjin ga kakarimasen
I've had an accident	事故をおこしました jee-kaw o o-kosh-ee-mash-ta jiko o okoshimashita

I've lost my car keys	車のカギをなくしました
	koo-roo-ma no kag-ee o
	  nak-shee-mash-ta
	kuruma no kagi o naku-
	  shimashita

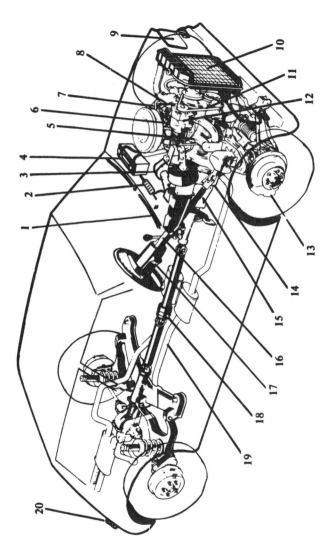

1	windshield wipers	ウインドスクリーンワイパー oo-een-doss-kreen-wye-pah uindosukurīn waipā
2	fuses	ヒューズ hughes hyūzu
3	heater	ヒーター hee-tah hitā
4	battery	バッテリー bat-tel-ee batterī
5	engine	エンジン en-jeen enjin
6	fuel pump	燃料ポンプ nen-ree-aw pomp-oo nenryō pompu
7	starter motor	スターター stah-tah sutātā

8	carburetor	キャブレター kee-ab-oo let-tah kyaburetā
9	lights	ライト lie-toh raito
10	radiator	ラジエーター laj-ee-air-tah rajiētā
11	fan belt	ファンベルト fam-bel-toh fanberuto
12	generator	ダイナモ die-nammo dainamo
13	brakes	ブレーキ bu-rair-kee burēki
14	clutch	クラッチ koo-lat-chee kuratchi

15	gear box	ギヤ・ボックス ghee-yaboks giyabokkusu
16	steering	ステアリング stay-arreen-goo sutearingu
17	ignition	点火装置 teng-kassaw-chee tenkasōchi
18	transmission	トランスミッション torranz-mee-shon toransumisshon
19	exhaust	排気筒 hike-ee-taw haikitō
20	indicators	ウインカー ween-kah uinkā

My car is...　私の車は……です
wattash-ee no koo-roo-ma wa...
　dess
watashi no kuruma wa...desu

　one kilometre away　1キロほどのところ
ee-chee kee-law hoddo no
　tokko-raw
ichi kiro hodo no tokoro

　three kilometres away　3キロほどのところ
san kee-law hoddo no tokko-raw
san kiro hodo no tokoro

Can you help me, please?　お願いできますか
on-eg-eye-dek-ee-mass-ka
onegai dekimasu ka

Do you do repairs?　修理をお願いできますか
shoo-ree o on-eg-eye dek-ee-mass
　ka
shūri o onegai dekimasu ka

I have a flat tire　パンクしました
pank-oo shee-mash-ta
panku shimashita

I have a broken windshield　フロントガラスがこわれました
foo-lon-toh gal-ass ga
　ko-warray-mash-ta
furonto garasu ga koware-
　mashita

I don't know what's wrong　どこが悪いのかわかりません
dokko ga warree no ka
　wak-arry-mass-en
doko ga warui no ka wakari-
　masen

I think the problem is here...　ここが悪いんだと思います
[*point*]

kokko ga wa-reen da tom-oy-mass
koko ga warui n da to omoimasu

Can you...　……していただけますか
...shtay ee-taddak-em-ass ka
...shite itadakemasu ka

　repair the fault?　故障個所を修理
kosh-aw kasho o shoo-ree
koshō kasho o shūri

come and look?	来て点検 kee-tay teng-ken kite tenken
estimate the cost?	費用の見積りを hee-aw no meet-soo-morree o hiyō no mitsumori o
Can you write it down?	書いていただけますか kye-tay ee-taddak-em-ass ka kaite itadakemasu ka
How long will the repair take?	修理にどのくらい時間がかかりますか shoo-ree nee donno goo-rye jee-kan ga kakka-ree-mass ka shūri ni dono gurai jikan ga kakarimasu ka
When will the car be ready?	いつ修理がおわりますか eet-soo shoo-ree ga o-warry-mass ka itsu shūri ga owarimasu ka
Can I see the bill?	請求書を見せてください say-kew-shaw o mee-set-ay koo-dass-eye seikyūsho o misete kudasai
This is my insurance document	これは保険証書です korray wa hokken shaw-shaw dess kore wa hoken shōsho desu

HIRING A CAR

Can I hire a car?	車を借りたいんですが koo-roo-ma o karry-tyne dess ga kuruma o karitai n desu ga
I need a car...	……車を借りたいんです ...koo-roo-ma o karry-tyne dess ...kuruma o karitai n desu
for two people	二人用の f-tarry yaw no futariyō no
for five people	五人用の go-neen yaw no goninyō no
for one day	1日 ee-chee nee-chee ichinichi

I need a car...
······車を借りたいんです
...koo-roo-ma o karry-tyne dess
...kuruma o karitai n desu

for five days
5日間
eet-skak-an
itsukakan

for a week
1週間
eesh-shoo kan
isshūkan

Can you write down...
······を書いていただけますか
...o kye-tay ee-taddak-em-ass ka
...o kaite itadakemasu ka

the deposit to pay?
保証金
hosh-aw-keen
hoshōkin

the charge per kilometre?
1キロ当りの料金
ee-chee kee-law atta-ree no ree
  aw-keen
ichikiro atari no ryōkin

the daily charge?
1日当りの料金
ee-chee nee-chee atta-ree no
  ree-aw-keen
ichinichi atari no ryōkin

the cost of insurance?
保険料
hokken ree-aw
hokenryō

Can I leave it in (Kyoto)?
（京都）で乗り捨てできますか
(kee-aw-toh)day norry-stay
  dek-ee-mass-ka
(kyōto) de norisute dekimasu ka

What documents do I need?
どんな書類が必要ですか
don-na shorroo-ee ga heet-soo-
  yaw dess ka
donna shorui ga hitsuyō desu ka

LIKELY REACTIONS

I don't do repairs

修理はやってないんです
shoo-ree wa yat-ten nine dess
shūri wa yatte nai n desu

Where's your car?

車はどこですか
koo-roo-ma wa dokko dess ka
kuruma wa doko desu ka

What make is it?

どこの車ですか
dokko no koo-roo-ma dess ka
doko no kuruma desu ka

Come back tomorrow/on Monday

あした 月曜日 来てください
ashta/gets-yaw-bee kee-tay
  koo-dass-eye
ashita/getsuyōbi kite kudasai

[*For days of the week, see p. 161*]

We don't hire cars

レンタカーはやってないんです
ren-tak-ah wa yat-tennine dess
rentakā wa yatte nai n desu

Your driver's license, please

運転免許証を見せてください
oon-ten menk yaw shaw o
  mee-set-ay koo-dass-eye
unten menkyoshō o misete
  kudasai

The mileage is unlimited

走行距離には制限がありません
saw-kaw kee-oree nee wa say-ghen
  ga arry-mass-en
sōkōkyori ni wa seigen ga
  arimasen

Public transport

ESSENTIAL INFORMATION

- Finding the way to the bus station, a bus stop, railway station and taxi stand, see p. 22.
- Using the public transport system is the fastest, cheapest and safest way to get around so you would do well to familiarize yourself with the overground and underground train systems in particular. City maps of these two systems (written in Roman letters) are available free of charge at major stations.
- All station names on platforms are written in Roman letters, and at each place you can see where you are, the station behind and the one ahead. The names of stations are also announced on the trains and buses just before you get there.
- Intercity travel on trains requires only that you purchase a ticket at the automatic vending machine (they give change). To determine the amount of the ticket you need only consult your Romanized map, compare it with the diagram in Japanese and count the number of stations you have to go.
- Not all trains stop at every station, so be sure to ask if yours does. You can work out if changing trains en route is necessary from your map.
- Long distance travel on the bullet train 新幹線 (sheen-kan-sen/shinkansen) and other trains requires that you get a boarding ticket 乗車券 (jaw-shak-en/jōshaken) and a special express ticket 特急券 (tok-yoo-ken/tokkyūken). If you want a reserved seat ask for a 指定席 (shtair-sek-ee/shiteiseki)—slightly more expensive but well worth it if you anticipate the train being crowded. Some trains have sleepers and diners for overnight trips.
- Buses are abundant but not as frequent as trains and can be very crowded during the rush hours. You get on most buses at the front, put your fare into the coin box on which is marked the one standard fare and get off at the rear. With some rural buses you get on at the rear, collect a ticket from a machine and pay the driver when you get off at the front. The fares here are based on the distance travelled. The driver will tell you how much you have to pay.
- You can flag taxis on the street or queue up at one of the stands

where they pick up passengers タクシー乗場 (tak-shee-norry-ba/ takushi noriba). It is always a good idea to have the address written in Japanese (your hotel can do this) and also a map if the place you are going to is not well known. For your return trip, carry a card with the name and location of your hotel, which most hotels provide. The driver opens and closes the left-hand rear door automatically, so *always* get out of the taxi on that side. Tipping is not necessary. A red light in the front window indicates that the taxi is available. A surcharge is payable between 11 p.m. and 5 a.m.

● Key words on signs: (see also p. 152)

国鉄	**(JNR**—Japanese National Railways)
私鉄	(private railways)
地下鉄/SUBWAY	(underground)
切符売場	(ticket vending)
駅	(station)
新幹線	(bullet train super-express)
バス	(bus)
タクシー乗場	(taxi stand)

WHAT TO SAY

Where do I buy a ticket?
切符売り場はどこですか
keep-poo oo-ree-ba wa dokko dess ka
kippu uriba wa doko desu ka

Where does the train for (Tokyo) leave from?
（東京）行きの電車はどこから出ますか
(tawk-yaw) yoo-kee no den-sha wa dokko karra dem-ass ka
(Tōkyō) yuki no densha wa doko kara demasu ka

At what time does the train leave for (Tokyo)?
（東京）行きの電車は何時に出ますか
(tawk-yaw) yoo-kee no den-sha wa nan-jee nee dem-ass-ka
(Tōkyō) yuki no densha wa nanji ni demasu ka

At what time does the train arrive in (Tokyo)?
電車は何時に（東京）に着きますか
den-sha wa nan-jee nee (tawk-yaw) neet-skee-mass ka
densha wa nanji ni (Tōkyō) ni tsukimasu ka

Is this the train for (Tokyo)?	これは（東京）行きの電車ですか
	korray wa (tawk-yaw) yoo-kee no den-sha dess ka
	kore wa (Tōkyō) yuki no densha desu ka
Where does the bus for (Kobe) leave from?	（神戸）行きのバスはどこから出ますか
	(kaw-bay) yoo-kee no bass wa dokko karra dem-ass ka
	(Kōbe) yuki no basu wa doko kara demasu ka
At what time does the bus leave for (Kobe)?	（神戸）行きのバスは何時に出ますか
	(kaw-bay) yoo-kee no bass wa nan-jee nee dem-ass ka
	(Kōbe) yuki no basu wa nanji ni demasu ka
At what time does the bus arrive at (Kobe)?	何時に（神戸）に着きますか
	nan-jee nee (kaw-bay) neet-skee-mass ka
	nanji ni (Kōbe) ni tsukimasu ka
Is this the bus for (Kobe)?	これは（神戸）行きのバスですか
	korray wa (kaw-bay) yoo-kee no bass dess ka
	kore wa (Kobe) yuki no basu desu ka
Do I have to change?	乗り換えないとだめですか
	norry-kye-en-eye-toh dam-ay dess ka
	norikaenai to dame desu ka
Where does...leave from?	……はどこから出ますか
	...wa dokko karra dem-ass ka
	...wa doko kara demasu ka
the bus	バス
	bass
	basu
the train	電車
	den-sha
	densha
the underground	地下鉄
	chee-kattets
	chikatetsu

[*Note that if you state the destination, the order of your sentence is: 1: destination 2: method of transport 3: question.*]

for the airport	空港への koo-kaw-ay no... kūkō e no
for the shrine	神社への jeen-ja-ay no... jinja e no
for the beach	海水浴場への kye-see-yok-oo jaw-ay no... kaisuiyokujō e no
for the market place	市への ee-chee-ay no... ichi e no
for the railway station	駅への ek-ee-ay no... eki e no
for the town centre	繁華街への han-kag-eye-ay no... hankagai e no
for the town hall	市役所への shee-ak-shaw-ay no... shiyakusho e no
for the temple	お寺への oterra-ay no... otera e no
for the swimming pool	プールへの poo-roo-ay no... pūru e no
Is this...	これは……ですか korray wa...dess ka kore wa...desu ka
the bus for the town centre?	繁華街へ行くバス han-kag-eye-ay eek-oo bass hankagai e iku basu
the monorail for the airport?	空港へ行くモノレール koo-kaw-ay eek-oo monno-rair-loo kūkō e iku monorēru
Where can I get a taxi?	タクシー乗り場はどこですか tak-shee norry-ba wa dokko dess ka takushī noriba wa doko desu ka
Can you put me off at the right stop, please?	着いたら教えてください tsee-tarra o-shee-ay-tay koo-dass-eye tsuitara oshiete kudasai

Can I book a seat?	席を予約できますか
	sek-ee o yoy-ak-oo dek-ee-mass ka
	seki o yoyaku dekimasu ka
A single	片道
	katta-mee-chee
	katamichi
A return	往復
	aw-f-koo
	ōfuku
First class	一等
	eet-taw
	ittō
Second class	二等
	nee-taw
	nitō
One adult	おとな一枚
	otonna ee-chee my
	otona ichimai
Two adults	おとな二枚
	otonna nee my
	otona nimai
and one child	と子ども一枚
	toh kod-ommo ee-chee my
	to kodomo ichimai
and two children	と子ども二枚
	toh kod-ommo nee my
	to kodomo nimai
How much is it?	いくらですか
	ee-koorra dess ka
	ikura desu ka

LIKELY REACTIONS

Over there	あそこです
	ass-okko dess
	asoko desu
Here	ここです
	kokko dess
	koko desu
Platform (1)	（1）番線
	(ee-chee) ban-sen
	(ichi) bansen

At (four) o'clock [*For times, see p. 158*]	（4）時です (yoj)-ee dess (yo-)ji desu
Change at (Shizuoka)	（静岡）で乗りかえてください (shee-zoo-awka) day norry-kye-et-ay koo-dass-eye (Shizuoka) de norikaete kudasai
Change at (the town hall)	（市役所）前で乗りかえてください (shee-ak-shaw) ma-air day norry-kye-et-ay koo-dass-eye (shiyakusho) mae de norikaete kudasai
This is your stop	ここでおりてください kokko day orree-tay koo-dass-eye koko de orite kudasai
There's only first class	一等だけです eet-taw dakked-ess ittō dake desu

Leisure

ESSENTIAL INFORMATION

- Finding the way to a place of entertainment, see p. 22.
- For times of day, see p. 158.
- Important signs, see p. 152.
- Most of the English-language newspapers and tabloids (some free of charge) carry information on leisure, entertainment, 'what's going on in town', etc. These guides are usually available at the larger hotels and at some bookshops and supermarkets (those that carry imported goods).
- Smoking is generally forbidden in all indoor places of public entertainment.

WHAT TO SAY

At what time does...open?	……は何時にあきますか	
	...wa nan-jee nee ak-ee mass ka	
	...wa nanji ni akimasu ka	
the art gallery	美術館	
	bee-joots-kan	
	bijutsukan	
the botanical garden	植物園	
	shok-oo-boots-en	
	shokubutsuen	
the cinema	映画館	
	ay-gak-an	
	eigakan	
the concert hall	コンサートホール	
	kon-sart haw-roo	
	konsāto hōru	
the disco	ディスコ	
	deess-ko	
	disuko	
the museum	博物館	
	hak-oo-boots-kan	
	hakubutsukan	
the night club	ナイトクラブ	
	nye-tok-rab-oo	
	naitokurabu	
the sports stadium	スタジアム	
	staj-ee-am-oo	
	sutajiamu	
the swimming pool	プール	
	poo-loo	
	pūru	
the theatre	劇場	
	ghek-ee-jaw	
	gekijō	
the zoo	動物園	
	daw-boots-oo-en	
	dōbutsuen	
At what time does...close?	……は何時にしまりますか	
	...wa nan-jee nee shee-marry-mass ka	
	...wa nanji ni shimarimasu ka	

the art gallery [*see above list*]	美術館 bee-joots-kan bijutsukan
At what time does...start?	……は何時にはじまりますか ...wa nan-jee nee haj-ee-marry- mass ka ...wa nanji ni hajimarimasu ka
the cabaret	キャバレー kee-abba-ray kyabarē
the concert	コンサート kon-sar-toh konsāto
the film	映画 ay-ga eiga
the match	試合 shee-eye shiai
the play	芝居 shib-eye shibai
the race	レース lairss-oo rēsu
How much is it...	……いくらですか ...ee-koorra dess ka ...ikura desu ka
for an adult/for a child?	おとなは　子どもは otonna wa/kod-ommo wa otona wa/kodomo wa
Two adults, please	おとな 二枚お願いします otonno nee-my on-eg-eye-shee- mass otona nimai onegai shimasu
Three children, please [*state price, if there's a choice*]	子ども 三枚お願いします kod-ommo san-my on-eg-eye- shee-mass kodomo sanmai onegai shimasu
Stalls/circle	一階席 二階席 eek-kye-sek-ee/nee-kye-sek-ee ikkaiseki/nikaiseki

Do you have...　　　　　　　……がありますか
　　　　　　　　　　　　　　...ga arry-mass ka
　　　　　　　　　　　　　　...ga arimasu ka

　a programme?　　　　　　プログラム
　　　　　　　　　　　　　　poo-rog-oo-ram-oo
　　　　　　　　　　　　　　puroguramu

　a guide book?　　　　　　案内書
　　　　　　　　　　　　　　an-nye-shaw
　　　　　　　　　　　　　　annaisho

Where is the toilet, please?　トイレはどこですか
　　　　　　　　　　　　　　toy-ray wa dokko dess ka
　　　　　　　　　　　　　　toire wa doko desu ka

Where is the cloakroom?　　クロークはどこですか
　　　　　　　　　　　　　　koo-raw-koo wa dokko dess ka
　　　　　　　　　　　　　　kurōku wa doko desu ka

I would like lessons in...　……を習いたいのですが
　　　　　　　　　　　　　　...o narrye-tye no dess ga
　　　　　　　　　　　　　　...o naraitai no desu ga

　sailing　　　　　　　　　ヨット
　　　　　　　　　　　　　　yot-toh
　　　　　　　　　　　　　　yotto

　skiing　　　　　　　　　スキー
　　　　　　　　　　　　　　skee
　　　　　　　　　　　　　　sukī

　water skiing　　　　　　水上スキー
　　　　　　　　　　　　　　see-jaw skee
　　　　　　　　　　　　　　suijō sukī

　wind-surfing　　　　　　ウインド・サーフィン
　　　　　　　　　　　　　　oo-een-doh sar-feen
　　　　　　　　　　　　　　uindo sāfin

　karate　　　　　　　　　空手
　　　　　　　　　　　　　　kalla-tay
　　　　　　　　　　　　　　karate

　flower arrangement　　　お花
　　　　　　　　　　　　　　o-hanna
　　　　　　　　　　　　　　ohana

　tea ceremony　　　　　　お茶
　　　　　　　　　　　　　　o-cha
　　　　　　　　　　　　　　ocha

　pottery　　　　　　　　焼き物
　　　　　　　　　　　　　　yak-ee-monno
　　　　　　　　　　　　　　yakimono

Can I rent...

……を借りたいのですが
...o karry-tye-no dess ga
...o karitai no desu ga

some skis?

スキー
skee
sukī

some skiboots?

スキーぐつ
skee-goo-tsoo
sukīgutsu

a boat?

ボート
baw-toh
bōto

a fishing rod?

つりざお
tsoo-ree-zao
tsurizao

a beach-chair?

ビーチ・チェア
bee-chee-chay-ah
bīchi chea

the necessary equipment?

必要なもの
sh-tsoo-yawn-ammonno
hitsuyō na mono

How much is it...

……いくらですか
...ee-koorra dess ka
...ikura desu ka

per day/per hour?

1日/1時間
ee-chee nee-chee/ee-chee jee-kan
ichinichi/ichijikan

Do I need a license?

免許がいりますか
men-kee-aw ga ee-ree mass ka
menkyo ga irimasu ka

Asking if things are allowed

WHAT TO SAY

Excuse me, please	すみません soo-mee-mass-en sumimasen
May one (lit. is it alright to)...	……いいですか ...ee dess ka ...ii desu ka
camp here?	キャンプしても kee-amp shtem-aw kyampu shite mo
come in?	はいっても height-tem-aw haitte mo
dance here?	ここで踊っても kokko dair oddot-em-aw koko de odotte mo
fish here?	ここで釣りをしても kokko dair tsoo-ree o shtem-aw koko de tsuri o shite mo
get out this way?	こっちから出ても ko-chee karra det-em-aw kotchi kara dete mo
leave one's things here?	荷物を置いておいても nee-mots o oy-toy-tem-aw nimotsu o oite oite mo
look around?	見ても mee-tem-aw mite mo
park here?	ここに駐車しても kokko nee choo-sha-shtem-aw koko ni chūsha shite mo
picnic here?	ここでお弁当を食べても kokko dair obent-aw o tabbet-em-aw koko de obentō o tabete mo
sit here?	ここに座っても kokko nee soo-wat-tem-aw koko ni suwatte mo
smoke here?	ここでタバコをすっても kokko dair tabbak-aw o s-tem-aw koko de tabako o sutte mo

swim here?	ここで泳いでも
	kokko dair oyoy-dem-aw
	koko de oyoide mo
take photos here?	ここで写真をとっても
	kokko dair sha-sheen o tot-tem-aw
	koko de shashin o totte mo
telephone here?	ここで電話をかけても
	kokko dair den-wa o kak-et-em-aw
	koko de denwa o kakete mo
wait here?	ここで待っても
	kokko-dair mat-tem-aw
	koko de matte mo

LIKELY REACTIONS

Yes, certainly	はい、いいですよ
	high ee dess yaw
	hai ii desu yo
Help yourself	どうぞ
	daw-zaw
	dōzo
I think so	いいと思います
	ee tom-oy-mass
	ii to omoimasu
Of course	もちろん
	motchee-ron
	mochiron
Yes, but be careful	はい、でも気をつけてください
	high demmo kee-o-tsket-ay koo-dass-eye
	hai,demo ki o tsukete kudasai
No, certainly not	いいえだめです
	ee-ay dam-ed-ess
	iie, dame desu
I don't think so	だめだと思います
	dam-ed-da-tom-oy-mass
	dame da to omoimasu
Not normally	ふつうはだめです
	f-tsoo wa dam-ed-ess
	futsū wa dame desu
Sorry	すみませんが
	soo-mee-mass-en ga
	sumimasen ga

Reference

PUBLIC NOTICES

● Signs for drivers, pedestrians, travelers, shoppers and overnight guests.

出発	Departure
到着	Arrivals
税関	Customs
受付	Reception
エレベーター	Elevator
エスカレーター	Escalator
入口	Entrance
出口	Exit
非常出口	Emergency exit
非常ブレーキ	Emergency brake
入場無料	Admission free
公衆電話	Public telephone
火災警報器	Fire alarm
引	Pull
押	Push
注意	Caution
禁止	Forbidden
立ち入り禁止	No trespassing
空き	Vacant (toilet)
使用中	Engaged (toilet)
お手洗/WC	Toilet
公衆便所	Public conveniences
女子用	Ladies
男子用	Gentlemen
浴室	Bathroom
救急	First aid
病院	Hospital
警察	Police
学校	School
遺失物	Lost property
手荷物預り所	Left luggage
コインロッカー	Luggage lockers
入	Slot, put in...
料金	Fees, charges

予約	Reserved
営業中	Open (for shops)
営業終了/閉店	Closed (for shops)
休業	Closed all day
営業時間	Opening hours
大売出し	Sale, clearance sale
売り切れ/満員御礼	Sold out, full house
セルフサービス	Self-service
会計	Cash desk
禁煙	No smoking
喫煙可	Smoking allowed
飲料水	Drinking water
案内所	Information office
案内	Guide
階	Floor
空室	Vacancies
貸室	Room to let
切符売場	Ticket office
寝台車	Sleeping car/sleeper
食堂車	Dining car
待合室	Waiting room
停留所	Bus-stop
高速道路	Motorway
危険	Danger
カーブ危険	Dangerous bend
二車線	Two-way traffic
追い越し禁止	Passing forbidden
侵入禁止	No entry
交差点	Crossroads
右側通行	Keep right
本線	Through traffic
通り抜け禁止	No through traffic
一方通行	One-way street
駐車禁止	No parking
駐車場	Car park
制限駐車区域	Restricted parking zone
行き止まり	Cul-de-sac
まわり道	Detour
信号	Traffic lights

Road closed

Minimum speed

Slow down

Stop

Stopping
permitted

NUMBERS
Cardinal numbers

0	ゼロ	zair-raw
		zero
		lay
		rei
		marroo
		maru
1	一 (つ)	ee-chee/shtots
		ichi/hitotsu
2	二 (つ)	nee/f-tats
		ni/futatsu
3	三 (つ)	san/meet-soo
		san/mittsu
4	四 (つ)	yon/shee/yot-soo
		yon/shi/yottsu
5	五 (つ)	gaw/eet-soot-soo
		go/itsutsu
6	六 (つ)	lok-oo/moot-soo
		roku/muttsu
7	七 (つ)	sh-chee/nan-at-soo
		shichi/nanatsu
8	八 (つ)	hatch-ee/yat-soo
		hachi/yattsu
9	九 (つ)	kew/kokko-not-soo
		kyū/kokonotsu
10	十	joo/taw
		jū/tŏ
11	十一	joo-ee-chee
		jūichi
12	十二	joo-nee
		jūni
13	十三	joo-san
		jūsan
14	十四	joo-yon
		jūyon
15	十五	joo-gaw
		jūgo
16	十六	joo-lok-oo
		jūroku
17	十七	joo-sh-chee/joo-nanna
		jūshichi

18	十八	joo-hatch-ee jūhachi
19	十九	joo-kew jūkyū
20	二十	nee-joo nijū
21	二十一	nee-joo-ee-chee nijūichi
22	二十二	nee-joo-nee nijūni
23	二十三	nee-joo-san nijūsan
24	二十四	nee-joo-yon nijūyon
25	二十五	nee-joo-gaw nijūgo
30	三十	san-joo sanjū
31	三十一	san-joo-ee-chee sanjūichi
35	三十五	san-joo-gaw sanjūgo
36	三十六	san-joo-lok-oo sanjūroku
37	三十七	san-joo-sh-chee sanjūshichi
38	三十八	san-joo-hatch-ee sanjūhachi
39	三十九	san-joo-kew sanjūkyū
40	四十	yon-joo yonjū
41	四十一	yon-joo-ee-chee yonjūichi
50	五十	gaw-joo gojū
51	五十一	gaw-joo-ee-chee gojūichi
60	六十	lok-oo-joo rokujū
61	六十一	lok-oo-joo-ee-chee rokujūichi

70	七十	nanna-joo
		nanajū
71	七十一	nanna-joo-ee-chee
		nanajūichi
80	八十	hatch-ee-joo
		hachijū
81	八十一	hatch-ee-joo-ee-chee
		hachijūichi
90	九十	kew-joo
		kyūjū
91	九十一	kew-joo-ee-chee
		kyūjūichi
100	百	h-yak-oo
		hyaku
101	百一	h-yak-oo-ee-chee
		hyakuichi
102	百二	h-yak-oo-nee
		hyakuni
125	百二十五	h-yak-oo-nee-joo-gaw
		hyakunijūgo
150	百五十	h-yak-oo-gaw-joo
		hyakugojū
175	百七十五	h-yak-oo-nanna-joo-gaw
		hyakunanajūgo
200	二百	nee-h-yak-oo
		nihyaku
250	二百五十	nee-h-yak-oo-gaw-joo
		nihyakugojū
300	三百	samb-yak-oo
		sambyakū
400	四百	yon-h-yak-oo
		yonhyaku
500	五百	gaw-h-yak-oo
		gohyaku
700	七百	nanna-h-yak-oo
		nanahyaku
1000	千	sen
		sen
1100	千百	sen-h-yak-oo
		senhyaku
2000	二千	nee-sen
		nisen
5000	五千	gaw-sen
		gosen

10000	一万	ee-chee-man
		ichiman
15000	一万五千	ee-chee-man-gaw-sen
		ichimangosen
20000	二万	nee-man
		niman
50000	五万	gaw-man
		goman
75000	七万五千	nanna-man-gaw-sen
		nanamangosen
100000	十万	joo-man
		jūman
500000	五十万	gaw-joo-man
		gojūman
1000000	百万	h-yak-oo-man
		hyakuman

Ordinal numbers

1st	一番目	ee-chee-ban-may
		ichibanme
2nd	二番目	nee-ban-may
		nibanme
3rd	三番目	sam-ban-may
		sanbanme
4th	四番目	yon-ban-may
		yonbanme
5th	五番目	gob-an-may
		gobanme
6th	六番目	lok-oo-ban-may
		rokubanme
7th	七番目	nanna-ban-may
		nanabanme
8th	八番目	hatch-ee-ban-may
		hachibanme
9th	九番目	kew-ban-may
		kyūbanme
10th	十番目	joo-ban-may
		jūbanme
11th	十一番目	joo-ee-chee-ban-may
		jūichibanme
12th	十二番目	joo-nee-ban-may
		jūnibanme

TIME

What time is it?	何時ですか nan-jee dess ka nanji desu ka
It's one o'clock	1時です ee-chee-jee dess ichiji desu
It's...	……です ...dess ...desu
two o'clock in the morning	朝の2時 assa-no nee-jee asa no niji
three o'clock in the afternoon	午後3時 goggo san-jee gogo sanji
four o'clock in the evening	夕方4時 yorroo-no yoj-ee yoru no kuji
nine o'clock in the morning	朝の9時 assa-no koo-jee asa no kuji
It's...	……です ...dess ...desu
noon	正午 shaw-go shōgo
midnight	夜中 yon-akka yonaka
It's...	……です ...dess ...desu
five past five	5時5分 goj-ee goffoon goji gofun
ten past five	5時10分 goj-ee jip-poon goji jippun
a quarter past five	5時15分 goj-ee joo-goffoon goji jūgofun

twenty past five	5時20分 goj-ee nee-jip-poon goji nijippun
twenty-five past five	5時25分 goj-ee nee-joo-goffoon goji nijūgofun
half past five	5時半 goj-ee han gojihan
twenty-five to six	6時25分前 lok-oo-jee nee-joo-goffoon ma-air rokuji nijūgofun mae
twenty to six	6時20分前 lok-oo-jee nee-jip-poon ma-air rokuji nijippun mae
a quarter to six	6時15分前 lok-oo-jee joo-goffoon-ma-air rokuji jūgofun mae
ten to six	6時10分前 lok-oo-jee jip-poon ma-air rokuji jippun mae
five to six	6時5分前 lok-oo-jee goffoon ma-air rokuji gofun mae
At what time...(does the train leave)?	電車は何時に出ますか den-sha wa nan-jee-nee dem-ass ka densha wa nanji ni demasu ka
At...	…… (に) です ...(nee) dess ...(ni) desu
13.00	13時 joo-san-jee jūsanji
14.05	14時5分 joo-yoj-ee goffoon jūyoji gofun
15.10	15時10分 joo-goj-ee jip-poon jūgoji jippun
16.15	16時15分 joo-lok-oo-jee joo-goffoon jūrokuji jūgofun

At...	……（に）です
	...(nee) dess
	...(ni) desu
17.20	17時20分
	joosh-chee-jee nee-jip-poon
	jūshichiji nijippun
18.25	18時25分
	joo-hatch-ee-jee nee-joo-goffoon
	jūhachiji nijūgofun
19.30	19時30分
	joo-koo-jee san-jip-poon
	jūkuji sanjippun
20.35	20時35分
	nee-joo-jee san-joo-goffoon
	nijūji sanjūgofun
21.40	21時40分
	nee-joo-ee-chee-jee yon-jip-poon
	nijūichiji yonjippun
22.45	22時45分
	nee-joo-nee-jee yon-joo-goffoon
	nijūniji yonjūgofun
23.50	23時50分
	nee-joo-san-jee goj-ip-poon
	nijūsanji gojippun
0.55	0時55分
	lay-jee goj-oo-goffoon
	reiji gojūgofun
in ten minutes	あと10分で
	atto jip-poon-dair
	ato jippun de
in a quarter of an hour	あと15分で
	atto joo-goffoon-dair
	ato jūgofun de
in half an hour	あと30分で
	atto san jip-poon-dair
	ato sanjippun de
in three quarters of an hour	あと45分で
	atto yon-joo-goffoon-dair
	ato yonjūgofun de

DAYS

Monday	月曜日 ghets-yaw-bee getsuyōbi
Tuesday	火曜日 ka-yaw-bee kayōbi
Wednesday	水曜日 see-yaw-bee suiyōbi
Thursday	木曜日 mok-oo-yaw-bee mokuyōbi
Friday	金曜日 keen-yaw-bee kinyōbi
Saturday	土曜日 doy-aw-bee doyōbi
Sunday	日曜日 nee-chee-aw-bee nichiyōbi
last Monday	先週の月曜日 sen-shoo no ghets-yaw-bee senshū no getsuyōbi
next Tuesday	来週の火曜日 lie-shoo no ka-yaw-bee raishū no kayōbi
on Wednesday	水曜日 （に） see-yaw-bee (nee) suiyōbi (ni)
on Thursdays	毎週木曜日 （に） my-shoo mok-oo-yaw-bee (nee) maishū mokuyōbi (ni)
until Friday	金曜日まで keen-yaw-bee madday kinyōbi made
before Saturday	土曜日のまえ doy-aw-bee no ma-air doyōbi no mae
after Sunday	日曜日のあと nee-chee-aw-bee no atto nichiyōbi no ato

the day before yesterday	おととい
	ottot-oy
	ototoi
two days ago	2日前
	f-tska ma-air
	futsuka mae
yesterday	きのう
	kee-naw
	kinō
yesterday morning	きのうの朝
	kee-naw no assa
	kinō no asa
yesterday afternoon	きのうの午後
	kee-naw no goggo
	kinō no gogo
last night (evening)	きのうの夜
	kee-naw no yorroo (ban)
	kinō no yoru (ban)
today	きょう
	kee-aw
	kyō
this morning	けさ
	kessa
	kesa
this afternoon	きょうの午後
	kee-aw no goggo
	kyō no gogo
tonight	今晩
	komban
	komban
tomorrow	あした
	ashta
	ashita
tomorrow morning	あしたの朝
	ashta no assa
	ashita no asa
tomorrow afternoon	あしたの午後
	ashta no goggo
	ashita no gogo
tomorrow evening/night	あしたの晩/夜
	ashta no ban/yorroo
	ashita no ban/yoru

the day after tomorrow	あさって
	ass-at-tay
	asatte

MONTHS AND DATES

January	一月
	ee-chee-gats
	ichigatsu
February	二月
	nee-gats
	nigatsu
March	三月
	san-gats
	sangatsu
April	四月
	shee-gats
	shigatsu
May	五月
	gog-ats
	gogatsu
June	六月
	lok-oo-gats
	rokugatsu
July	七月
	sh-chee-gats
	shichigatsu
August	八月
	hatch-ee-gats
	hachigatsu
September	九月
	koo-gats
	kugatsu
October	十月
	joo-gats
	jūgatsu
November	十一月
	joo-ee-chee-gats
	jūichigatsu
December	十二月
	joo-nee-gats
	jūnigatsu

in January	一月に ee-chee-gats nee ichigatsu ni
until February	二月まで nee-gats madday nigatsu made
before March	三月の前 san-gats no ma-air sangatsu no mae
after April	四月以降 shee-gats ee-kaw shigatsu ikō
during May	五月中 gog-ats-chew gogatsuchū
the beginning of July	七月のはじめ sh-chee-gats no haj-ee-may shichigatsu no hajime
the middle of August	八月半ば hatchee-gats nak-abba hachigatsu nakaba
the end of September	九月の末 koo-gats no swair kugatsu no sue
last month	先月 sen-gets sengetsu
this month	今月 kon-gets kongetsu
next month	来月 lie-gets raigetsu
in spring	春に harroo nee haru ni
in summer	夏に nat-soo nee natsu ni
in autumn	秋に ak-ee nee aki ni

in winter	冬に foo-yoo nee fuyu ni
this year	今年 kottosh-ee kotoshi
last year	去年 kee-yonnen kyonen
next year	来年 lie-nen rainen
in 1984	1984年に sen-kew-h-yak-oo hatch-ee-joo- 　yonnen nee senkyūhyaku-hachijūyonen ni
in 1988	1988年に sen-kew-h-yak-oo hatch-ee-joo- 　hatch-ee-nen nee senkyūhyaku-hachijūhachinen ni
in 1990	1990年に sen-kew-h-yak-oo kew-joo-nen 　nee senkyūhyakukyūjūnen ni
What's the date today?	きょうは何日ですか kee-aw wa nan-nee-chee dess ka kyō wa nannichi desu ka

(A special counting system is used for the first ten, the fourteenth and the twentieth days of the month.)

It's...	……です ...dess ...desu
the first	一日 tsee-tatch-ee tsuitachi
the second	二日 f-tska futsuka
the third	三日 meek-ka mikka

It's... ......です

... dess
... desu

the fourth 四日
yok-ka
yokka

the fifth 五日
eets-ka
itsuka

the sixth 六日
mwee-ka
muika

the seventh 七日
nan-aw-ka
nanoka

the eighth 八日
yaw-ka
yōka

the ninth 九日
kokko-nokka
kokonoka

the tenth 十日
taw-ka
tōka

the eleventh 十一日
joo-ee-chee-nee-chee
jūichinichi

the twelfth 十二日
joo-nee-nee-chee
jūninichi

the fourteenth 十四日
joo-yok-ka
jūyokka

the twentieth 二十日
hats-ka
hatsuka

the twenty-first 二十一日
nee-joo-ee-chee-nee-chee
nijūichinichi

the twenty-fifth 二十五日
nee-joo-gonnee-chee
nijūgonichi

the thirtieth	三十日 san-joo-nee-chee sanjūnichi
the 6th of March	三月六日 san-gats mwee-ka sangatsu muika
the 12th of April	四月十二日 shee-gats joo-nee-nee-chee shigatsu jūninichi
the 21st of August	八月二十一日 hatch-ee-gats nee-joo-ee-chee-nee- chee hachigatsu nijūichinichi

Public holidays

● On these days, offices and schools are closed.

1 January	元日	New Year's Day
15 January	成人の日	Adults' Day
11 February	建国記念日	National Foundation Day
21 March	春分の日	Vernal Equinox Day
29 April	天皇誕生日	Emperor's Birthday
3 May	憲法記念日	Constitution Memorial Day
5 May	子どもの日	Children's Day
15 September	敬老の日	Respect for the Aged Day
23 September	秋分の日	Autumnal Equinox Day
10 October	体育の日	Sports Day
3 November	文化の日	Culture Day
23 November	勤労感謝の日	Labour Thanksgiving Day

COUNTRIES AND NATIONALITIES
Countries

Australia	オーストラリア
	awss-taw-rall-ya
	ōsutoraria
Austria	オーストリア
	awss-taw-ree-a
	ōsutoria
Belgium	ベルギー
	berroo-ghee
	berugī
Canada	カナダ
	kann-adda
	kanada
Czech Republic	チェコスロバキア
	chek-oss-lobbak-ya
	chekosurobakia
Denmark	デンマーク
	den-mark-oo
	denmāku
Eire/Ireland	アイルランド
	eye-lando
	airurando
England ⎤ Britain ⎦	イギリス
	ee-ghee-reess
	igirisu
Finland	フィンランド
	feen-lando
	fuinrando
France	フランス
	frannsser
	furansu
Germany	ドイツ
	doyts
	doitsu
Greece	ギリシア
	ghirreesh-ya
	girishia
India	インド
	eendo
	indo

Italy	イタリア
	ee-tal-ya
	itaria
Netherlands]	オランダ
Holland]	oll-anda
	oranda
New Zealand	ニュージーランド
	new-jee-lando
	nyūjīrando
Norway	ノルウェー
	norroo-air
	noruwē
Pakistan	パキスタン
	pak-ee-stan
	pakisutan
Poland	ポーランド
	paw-lando
	pōrando
Portugal	ポルトガル
	porroo-tog-alloo
	porutogaru
Russia	ソ連
	saw-ren
	soren
Scotland	スコットランド
	skot-tol-ando
	sukottorando
South Africa	南アフリカ
	mee-nam-ee aff-ree-ka
	minami afurika
Spain	スペイン
	spain
	supein
Sweden	スウェーデン
	swair-denn
	suēden
Switzerland	スイス
	soo-eess
	suisu
United Kingdom	英国
	ay-kok-oo
	eikoku

United States	アメリカ（合衆国） am-ellee-ka (gash-shoo-kok-oo) amerika (gasshūkoku)
Wales	ウェールズ wair-rooz uēruzu
Yugoslavia	ユーゴスラビア yoo-goss-labb-ya yūgosurabia

Nationalities

American	アメリカ人 am-ellee-kajeen amerikajin
Australian	オーストラリア人 awss-taw-rall-yajeen ōsutorariajin
British	英国人 ay-kok-oo-jeen eikokujin
Canadian	カナダ人 kann-adda-jeen kanadajin
English	イギリス人 ee-ghee-reesser-jeen igirisujin
Indian	インド人 eendo-jeen indojin
Irish	アイルランド人 eye-lando-jeen airurandojin
a New Zealander	ニュージーランド人 new-jee-lando-jeen nyūjīrandojin
a Pakistani	パキスタン人 pak-ee-stan-jeen pakisutanjin

Scottish	スコットランド人
	skot-tol-ando-jeen
	sukottorandojin
Welsh	ウェールズ人
	wair-rooz-jeen
	uēruzujin

DEPARTMENT STORE GUIDE

オーディオ製品	Audio products
ベビー服	Babywear
地階	Basement
寝具	Bedding
ベルト	Belts
毛布	Blankets
書籍	Books
キャンプ用品	Camping
カー用品	Car accessories
カーペット	Carpets
会計	Cash desk
子供用品	Child/children
陶磁器	China
清掃用品	Cleaning materials
化粧品	Cosmetics
美術工芸品	Crafts
クレジット	Credit-accounts
カーテン	Curtains
クッション	Cushions
お惣菜	Delicatessen
日曜大工	Do-it-yourself
電化製品	Electrical appliances
布地	Fabrics
ファッション小物	Fashion accessories
2階	First floor
食料品	Food
冷凍食品	Frozen food
家具	Furniture
贈答品	Gifts

ガラス食器	Glassware
1階	Ground floor
メンズ小物	Haberdashery
金物	Hardware
案内所	Information
インテリア	Interior decoration
宝飾品	Jewelry
台所用品	Kitchen tools
ニットウェア	Knitwear
皮革製品	Leather goods
照明	Lighting
紳士服	Men's wear
事務用品	Office supplies
香水	Perfumery
写真	Photography
ラジオ	Radio
既製服	Ready-to-wear
レコード	Records
3階	Second floor
シャツ	Shirts
靴	Shoes
スリッパ	Slippers
スポーツ用品	Sports articles
文房具	Stationery
ストッキング	Stockings
テレビ	Television
ネクタイ	Ties
喫煙具	Tobacco, pipes and cigarettes
洗面用具	Toiletries
玩具	Toys
旅行用品	Travel articles
下着	Underwear
婦人用下着	Women's underwear
婦人服	Women's wear

CONVERSION TABLES

Read the centre column of these tables from right to left to convert
from metric to imperial and from left to right to convert from
imperial to metric e.g. 5 litres = 8.80 pints; 5 pints = 2.84 litres

pints		litres		gallons		litres
1.76	1	0.57		0.22	1	4.55
3.52	2	1.14		0.44	2	9.09
5.28	3	1.70		0.66	3	13.64
7.07	4	2.27		0.88	4	18.18
8.80	5	2.84		1.00	5	22.73
10.56	6	3.41		1.32	6	27.28
12.32	7	3.98		1.54	7	31.82
14.08	8	4.55		1.76	8	36.37
15.84	9	5.11		1.98	9	40.91

ounces		grams		pounds		kilos
0.04	1	28.35		2.20	1	0.45
0.07	2	56.70		4.41	2	0.91
0.11	3	85.05		6.61	3	1.36
0.14	4	113.40		8.82	4	1.81
0.18	5	141.75		11.02	5	2.27
0.21	6	170.10		13.23	6	2.72
0.25	7	198.45		15.43	7	3.18
0.28	8	226.80		17.64	8	3.63
0.32	9	255.15		19.84	9	4.08

inches		centimetres		yards		metres
0.39	1	2.54		1.09	1	0.91
0.79	2	5.08		2.19	2	1.83
1.18	3	7.62		3.28	3	2.74
1.58	4	10.16		4.37	4	3.66
1.95	5	12.70		5.47	5	4.57
2.36	6	15.24		6.56	6	5.49
2.76	7	17.78		7.66	7	6.40
3.15	8	20.32		8.65	8	7.32
3.54	9	22.86		9.84	9	8.23

miles		kilometres
0.62	1	1.61
1.24	2	3.22
1.86	3	4.83
2.49	4	6.44
3.11	5	8.05
3.73	6	9.66
4.35	7	11.27
4.97	8	12.87
5.59	9	14.48

A quick way to convert kilometres to miles: divide by 8 and multiply by 5. To convert miles to kilometres: divide by 5 and multiply by 8.

fahrenheit (°F)	centigrade (°C)		lbs/ sq in	k/ sq cm
212°	100°	boiling point	18	1.3
100°	38°		20	1.4
98.4°	36.9°	body temperature	22	1.5
86°	30°		25	1.7
77°	25°		29	2.0
68°	20°		32	2.3
59°	15°		35	2.5
50°	10°		36	2.5
41°	5°		39	2.7
32°	0°	freezing point	40	2.8
14°	−10°		43	3.0
−4°	−20°		45	3.2
			46	3.2
			50	3.5
			60	4.2

To convert °C to °F, divide by 5, multiply by 9 and add 32.
To convert °F to °C, take away 32, divide by 9 and multiply by 5.

CLOTHING SIZES

Remember, always try on clothes before buying. Clothing sizes are usually unreliable.

women's dresses and suits

UK	32	34	36	38	40	42
USA	10	12	14	16	18	20
JAPAN	9	11	13	15	17	19

men's suits and coats

UK and USA	36	38	40	42	44	46
JAPAN		90	95	100	105	110	115

men's shirts

UK and USA	15	16	17	18
JAPAN	38	41	43	45

stockings and socks

UK and USA	8	8½	9	9½	10	10½	11	11½
JAPAN		20	21	22	23	24	25	26	27

shoes

UK	5	6	7	8	9	10	11
USA	6½	7½	8½	9½	10½	11½	12½
JAPAN	23	24	25	26	27	28	29

Do it yourself
Some notes on the language

This section does not deal with 'grammar' as such. The purpose here is to explain some of the most obvious and elementary nuts and bolts of the language, based on the principal phrases included in the book. This information should enable you to produce more sentences of your own making.

- In speaking Japanese, you do not have many of the problems encountered in European languages such as articles (a, an, the etc.), cases (accusative, genitive etc.), gender (masculine, feminine, neuter) or words like 'some', 'any' etc. These grammatical features either do not exist or are hardly ever used in the colloquial language.
- Neither is there usually any difference between singular and plural forms. You can say その本をください (sonno hon o koo-dass-eye/sono hon o kudasai) for 'give me that book' or 'give me those books'. Singularity or plurality is usually clear from the context of the sentence.

COUNTING

Obviously, when shopping, you need to be specific, and in such cases the Japanese language can be just that:

three tickets, please
きっぷを3枚ください
keep-poo o *san-my* koo-dass-eye
kippu o *sanmai* kudasai

four lettuces, please
レタスを4つください
let-ass o *yot-soo* koo-dass-eye
retasu o *yottsu* kudasai

The problem here is that numbers in Japanese are hardly ever independent entities; they are always conditioned by the shape of the nouns they go with:

san-bon	3 long cylindrical things (e.g. pencils, trains)
sanbon	三本
san-my	3 flat things (e.g. tickets, paper)
sanmai	三枚
san-bikky	3 small living things (insects, birds)
sanbiki	三匹

三個	san-kaw sanko	3 solid objects, not too large (apples, pottery)
三人	san-neen sannin	3 people
三冊	san-sats sansatsu	3 books

There are many more such counters, but you need not despair. Their number is slowly decreasing, and the ones above are perhaps the most common counters you will need to recognize. In making your own sentences however, you can get round the problem by using just one group of counters, which will be understood by any Japanese:

1	ひとつ	shtots hitotsu
2	ふたつ	f-tats futatsu
3	三つ	meet-soo mittsu
4	四つ	yot-soo yottsu
5	五つ	eet-soot-soo itsutsu
6	六つ	moot-soo muttsu
7	七つ	nannat-soo nanatsu
8	八つ	yat-soo yattsu
9	九つ	kokko-not-soo kokonotsu
10	十	taw tō

For more than ten you just continue with the usual counting system for cardinal numbers already mentioned (see p. 154). But remember that cardinal numbers between 1 and 10 are used on their own only in mathematical calculations as a rule and not to count objects.

To summarize:

For 'people' there is a special counter which is furthermore irregular for fewer than 3:

one person	一人
	sh-torry
	hitori

two people	二人
	f-tarry
	futari

three people	三人
	san-neen
	sannin

four people	四人
	yonneen
	yonin

seven people	七人
	sh-chee-neen
	shichinin

Objects have their own regular counters but the general system listed above (shtots, f-tats etc.) can be used instead.

one book	本 ·冊　　本ひとつ
	hon eess-sats *or* hon shtots
	hon issatsu *or* hon hitotsu

two books	本 二冊　　本ふたつ
	hon nee-sats *or* hon f-tats
	hon nisatsu *or* hon futatsu

three books	本 三冊　　本 三つ
	hon san-sats *or* hon meet-soo
	hon sansatsu *or* hon mittsu

one ticket	切符 ·枚　　切符ひとつ
	keep-poo ee-chee-my *or* keep-poo sh-tots
	kippu ichimai *or* kippu hitotsu

three tickets	切符三枚　　切符三つ keep-poo san-my *or* keep-poo meet-soo kippu sanmai *or* kippu mittsu
one loaf of bread	パン一個　　パンひとつ pan eek-kaw *or* pan shtots pan ikko *or* pan hitotsu
two loaves of bread	パン二個　　パンふたつ pan nee-kaw *or* pan f-tats pan niko *or* pan futatsu

TENSES

The Japanese tense system is very simple, consisting essentially of only present (dess/desu; mass/masu) and past forms (deshta/deshita; mashta/mashita). For the future you simply use a preposition of time with the present tense e.g.

I will go tomorrow	あした行きます ashta ee-kee-mass ashita ikimasu
I'm going to go next week	来週行きます lie-shoo ee-kee-mass raishū ikimasu
I'm going at 3 o'clock	3時に行きます san-jee-nee ee-kee-mass sanji ni ikimasu

With all tenses the verb is usually at the end of the sentence.

PARTICLES

The most important element of basic Japanese is perhaps the particle, which indicates whether something is the subject or object of the sentence. One could just about be understood by omitting these particles, but to avoid misunderstandings it is best to remember them.

subject particle	は wa wa
emphatic subject particle	が ga (also used to link numerous idiomatic expressions) ga

direct object particle	を
	o
	o
question particle	か
	ka
	ka

Particles indicating movement or place:

to		へ
		ay
		e
	or	に
		nee
		ni
from		から
		karra
		kara
at		で
		dair
		de
in		に
		nee
		ni
as far as/until		まで
		madday
		made

What is your name?	お名前はなんですか
(lit: as for (your) name what is (it)?)	onna-my *wa* nan dess *ka*
	onamae *wa* nan desu *ka*
Is it alright to fish here?	ここで釣りをしてもいいですか
(lit: here *at* fishing is (it) alright?)	kokko *dair* tsoo-ree *o* shtem-aw ee-dess *ka*
	koko *de* tsuri *o* shite mo ii desu *ka*
I'm staying in Harumi St.	晴海通りにいます
(lit: Harumi St. *in* (I) am)	harroo-mee daw-ree *nee* ee-mass
	harumi-dōri *ni* imasu
I'm from London/I've come from London	私はロンドンから来ました
(lit: I London *from* came)	wattash-ee wa lon-don *karra* kee-mash-ta
	watashi wa rondon *kara* kimashita
I'll wait until 3 o'clock	3時まで待ちます
(lit: 3 o'clock *until* (I will) wait)	san-jee *madday* match-ee-mass
	sanji *made* machimasu

THIS AND THAT

Japanese distinguishes between things very close to the speaker これ korray/kore (this, these), things at an intermediate distance away from the speaker それ sorray/sore (that, those, it, them) and things further away from the speaker, over there あれ array/are (that, those, it, them over there). The same distinction applies when the words 'this', 'that', 'these', 'those' are placed before nouns この本 konno hon/kono hon(this book here)その本 sonno hon/sono hon (that book there) あの本 anno hon/ano hon (that book over there). The context of the sentence is all-important in deciding whether to use それ sorray/sore or あれ array/are.

PRONOUNS

Personal pronouns are often omitted in Japanese, which again depends on context for understanding who is referring to whom or to what. The first person pronoun 私 /wattash-ee/watashi is usually omitted.

where are (you) going?	どこへ行きますか
(lit: where to going?)	dokko ay ee-kee-mass ka
	doko e ikimasu ka
(I'm) going to the station	駅へ行きます
(lit: station to going)	ek-ee ay ee-kee-mass
	eki e ikimasu

It's only necessary to use personal pronouns when to omit them would cause confusion e.g. *he* wants a beer and *I'll* have a glass of wine.

彼はビールで、私はグラスワインを
ください

karray wa bee-roo dair *wattash-ee*
wa goo-rass wa-een o koo-dass-
eye

kare wa bīru de *watashi* wa
gurasu wain o kudasai

HELPING OTHERS

You can help yourself with phrases such as:

I'd like...a sandwich	サンドイッチをください
	sando-ee-chee o koo-dass-eye
	sandoitchi o kudasai
Where can I buy...a news-paper?	新聞はどこで買えますか
	sheem-boon wa dokko dair ka-em-ass ka
	shimbun wa doko de kaemasu ka

I need a receipt	領収書がほしいんですが ree-aw-shoo-shaw ga hosh-een dess ga ryōshūsho ga hoshii n desu ga 領収書をお願いします ree-aw-shoo-shaw o on-eg-eye-shee-mass ryōshūsho o onegai shimasu

If you come across a compatriot having trouble making himself or herself understood, you should be able to speak to the Japanese on their behalf. This you can do in two ways. Either by omitting pronouns and putting one of the following two phrases at the end of the sentence:

(he/she/they/we/) is/are saying...	……といっています ...taw eet-tay-ee-mass ...to itte imasu
(he/she/they/we) is/are asking...	……ときいています ...taw kee-tay-ee-mass ...to kiite imasu

In the latter case, ときいていますtaw kee-tay-ee-mass/to kiite imasu refers to a question seeking information such as 'what time does the train leave?' If the compatriot is trying to make a request (can I have a sandwich etc.) you must add the phraseとお願いしていますtaw on-eg-eye shtay-ee-mass/to onegai shite imasu (he/she/they/we) is/are requesting.

Or, if you prefer to use pronouns, you simply put them at the head of the sentence:

He'd like a sandwich	彼はサンドイッチがほしいんです *karray* wa sando-ee-chee ga hosh-een dess *kare* wa sandoitchi ga hoshii n desu
She'd like a sandwich	彼女はサンドイッチがほしいんです *kanno-jaw* wa sando-ee-chee ga hosh-een dess *kanojo* wa sandoitchi ga hoshii n desu
Where can *he* buy a newspaper?	彼はどこで新聞が買えますか *karray* wa dokko dair sheem-boon ga ka-em-ass ka *kare* wa doko de shimbun ga kaemasu ka

Where can *she* buy a news-paper?	彼女はどこで新聞が買えますか *kanno-jaw* wa dokko dair sheem-boon ga ka-em-ass ka *kanojo* wa doko de shimbun ga kaemasu ka
He needs a receipt	彼は領収書がほしいんです *karray* wa ree-aw-shoo-shaw ga hosh-een dess *kare* wa ryōshūsho ga hoshii n desu
She needs a receipt	彼女は領収書がほしいんです *kanno-jaw* wa ree-aw-shoo-shaw ga hosh-een dess *kanojo* wa ryōshūsho ga hoshii n desu

To help a couple or a group in difficulties, the Japanese words for 'they' are 彼ら kal-ella/karera for men and 彼女ら kanno-jorra/kanojora for women.

They'd like some cheese	彼らはチーズがほしいんです *kal-ella* wa cheez ga hosh-een dess *karera* wa chīzu ga hoshii n desu
Where can *they* get some aspirin?	彼女らはどこでアスピリンが買えますか *kanno-jorra* wa dokko dair ass-pee-leen ga ka-em-ass ka *kanojora wa doko de asupirin ga kaemasu ka*
They need some water	彼らは水がいります *kal-ella* wa mee-zoo ga ee-lee-mass *karera* wa mizu ga irimasu

If the group is made up of both men and women, use the 'kal-ella/karera' form.

What about two of you? The word for 'we' is 私たち wattash tatch-ee/watashitachi.

We'd like some wine	私たちはワインがほしいんです *wattash-tatch-ee* wa wye-een ga hosh-een dess *watashitachi* wa wain ga hoshii n desu

Where can *we* buy some aspirin?	私たちはどこでアスピリンが買えますか *wattash-tatch-ee* wa dokko dair ass-pee-leen ga ka-em-ass ka *watashitachi* wa doko de asupirin ga kaemasu ka
We need a beer	私たちはビールがほしいんです *wattash-tatch-ee* wa bee-roo ga hosh-een dess *watashitachi* wa bīru ga hoshii n desu

GET

The useful and all-purpose word 'get' does not exist as such in Japanese. You have to be more specific when you want to translate the word. Do you, for example, mean 'buy' or 'receive', 'find' or 'come into contact with', 'pick up' or 'get on'? Consider the following examples:

Where can I get a newspaper? (i.e. buy one)	新聞はどこで買えますか sheem-boon wa dokko dair *ka-em-ass* ka shimbun wa doko de *kaemasu* ka
Do we get a glass of water? (i.e. receive one)	水をいただけますか mee-zoo o *ee-taddak-em-ass* ka mizu o *itadakemasu* ka
Where can I get a bus to the hotel? (i.e. where does the bus to the hotel *leave from*?	ホテル行きのバスはどこから出ますか ho-terroo yoo-kee no bass wa dokko karra *dem*-ass ka hoteru yuki no **basu** wa doko kara demasu ka (where does the hotel bus leave from?)
Where can I get the key? (i.e. pick it up)	カギはどこでもらえますか kag-ee wa dokko dair *mor-eye-em-ass ka* kagi wa doko de *moraemasu ka*
I want to get to a campsite (i.e. go to one)	キャンプ場に行きたいんです kee-amp-jaw nee *ee-kee-tine dess* kyampujō ni *ikitai n desu*

MORE PRACTICE

Here are some more Japanese names of things. See how many different sentences you can make up, using the various points of information given earlier in this section.

ashtray	灰皿
	high-zarra
	haizara
bag	バッグ
	bag-goo
	baggu
brush	ブラシ
	boo-rash-ee
	burashi
calculator	計算機
	kay-san-kee
	keisanki
car	車
	koo-roo-mah
	kuruma
dentist	歯医者
	high-sha
	haisha
fruit	くだもの
	koo-dam-onno
	kudamono
glass	グラス
	goo-lass
	gurasu
ice cream	アイスクリーム
	eyess-koo-reem-oo
	aisukurīmu
melon	メロン
	mel-on
	meron
postcard	はがき
	hag-akky
	hagaki
raincoat	レインコート
	lairn-kaw-taw
	reinkōto

salad	サラダ
	sal-adda
	sarada
soap	石けん
	sek-ken
	sekken
sunglasses	サングラス
	san-glass-oo
	sangurasu
tape-recorder	テープレコーダー
	tair-prek-aw-da
	tēpurekōda
ticket	切符
	keep-poo
	kippu
tomato	トマト
	tom-atto
	tomato
wallet	さいふ
	sye-foo
	saifu
watch	時計
	tok-air
	tokei

Index